Blockchain Hurricane

Blockchain Hurricane

Origins, Applications, and Future of Blockchain and Cryptocurrency

Kate Baucherel

For Glenn

Fellow explorers in the
world - and universe -
of tech.

Kate Baucherel
    November 2020

 BUSINESS EXPERT PRESS

First published in 2020 by
Business Expert Press, LLC
222 East 46th Street, New York, NY 10017
www.businessexpertpress.com

ISBN-13: 978-1-95152-736-5 (paperback)
ISBN-13: 978-1-95152-737-2 (e-book)

Business Expert Press Finance and Financial Management Collection

Collection ISSN: 2331-0049 (print)
Collection ISSN: 2331-0057 (electronic)

Cover and interior design by Exeter Premedia Services Private Ltd., Chennai, India

First edition: 2020

10 9 8 7 6 5 4 3 2 1

Printed in the United States of America.

Endorsements

"This is a brilliant read. It is beautifully written with authenticity, clarity and conceptual elegance. Explanations are clear and engaging, making it an indispensable and accessible resource for those wishing to gain in or reinforce fundamental understanding; developmental origins are painstakingly and generously elaborated; and challenges for future developers and adopters are both appetizing and pull no punches. I have previously sought to read about this topic but never yet come across such a readable, uncluttered, informative, measured and engaging exposition. Superb."

Prof. Alison Shaw, Newcastle University

"There is no question that Blockchain is a technology that will disrupt a number of industries, including the insurance industry. It is disruptive not only because the technology is by nature groundbreaking but also because it brings together parties that in the past would have been in competition or in some sort of conflict, for the benefit of transparency and simplification, and in fine, to provide the best possible outcome for customers. This book does an excellent job at explaining why, and how, this will be the case."

Hélène Stanway, Digital Leader, AXA XL

Abstract

The hype around blockchain technology is matched only by the innovation it inspires and the skepticism it provokes. This book gives business decision makers and students a clear overview of the history, current applications, and future potential of distributed ledgers and cryptocurrency. It explores strengths and weaknesses, emerging opportunities, and perceived threats. Technical frameworks are presented in a business context to help strategists understand the risks and rewards of different approaches to blockchain implementation, and the decision factors in determining whether this is a viable solution to the problem at hand.

Keywords

blockchain; cryptocurrency; distributed ledger; bitcoin, ethereum; hyperledger; permissioned; private; decentralized; decentralization

Contents

Acknowledgments

Writing this book has been fun, eye-opening, surprising, and occasionally frustrating. Thank you to all the people who have told me their remarkable stories, answered far-reaching and sometimes daft questions one-on-one and in open forums, and opened up new avenues for me to explore as I descended deeper into the rabbit hole. Both before and during the writing process I learned a huge amount from long conversations, inspiring speeches, roundtable discussions, chats over beer, and lengthy message exchanges with hugely talented blockchain practitioners from all corners of the world. I am incredibly grateful to all of you for taking the time to answer questions and tell me about your work, and for checking the accuracy of how our conversations are reflected in this text. Thanks to Gabby Dizon, Patricia O'Callaghan, Alex Amsel, Adam Clarey, Paul Miller, Rachel Wolfson, Anne Puck, Dylan Jones, Dan Lyons, Caitlin Long, Tyler Lindholm, Joshua Ashley Klayman, Ian Cornwell, Mark Bell, Martin Bartlam, Kim Cope, Jeremy Gardner, Tom Kysar, Hélène Stanway, Ghanshyam Patil, Mike Smith, Ant Stevens, Adryenn Ashley, Hartej Sawhney, Mariam Turashvili, Steve Schneider, Anne Ahola Ward, Daniel Doll-Steinberg, Tonya Evans, Corey Segall, Shontavia Johnson, Graham Richter, Helen Disney, Genevieve Leveille, Terence Eden, Rich Julien, Jeff Hasselman, Kapil Dhar, Aad van Moorsel, Holly Burgess, Josh Edwards, Thomas Power, Jonny Fry, Andreas Antonopolous, Marguerite deCourcelle, Emily Rose Dallara, and Akane Yokoo. Special thanks to Alison Shaw, Paul Sitoh, Steve Blanks, David Morton, and Joanne Rout for proofreading and suggesting changes, additions, and clarifications. I've also had a lot of encouragement along the way from friends, colleagues, the team at Business Expert Press, and of course, my family. My thanks and love to Xavier, Gaelle and Loïc for your patience and support, always.

CHAPTER 1

The Hype and the Hope

What has blockchain ever done for us? Its first decade has been turbulent, fascinating, full of promise, fraught with danger, riddled with duplicity, and ultimately inspiring. Its inextricable link to Bitcoin has generated a high degree of skepticism over the contribution blockchain can make to our world, matched only by the fervor of advocates who believe that blockchain and cryptocurrency can drive fundamental changes in working practices and meet societal challenges.

This book seeks to inform, not to evangelize. We will look at the evolution of cryptocurrency from its origins in cryptography to its birth in the fires of a global financial crisis, and through the first decade of digital cash. We will examine the niches where blockchain, the technology that underpins cryptocurrency, can be an effective solution to other problems, where it is already being employed, and how to decide whether it is an appropriate path to take in resolving challenges in your business and industry. We'll reflect on the mistakes that have been made in rushing to adopt blockchain where hype overtakes practicality, in the hope that we can learn from a checkered history. We'll also explore the real innovations that are happening, the things that could not be achieved without blockchain and cryptocurrency, and the future impact that experts foresee.

Decrypting the Jargon

One of the challenges of any emerging technology is the new vocabulary that develops to explain its features. The jargon surrounding blockchain and cryptocurrency is no exception.

Blockchain is technically a subset of Distributed Ledger Technology (DLT), but the term has become ubiquitous. Due to common misconceptions and a lack of trust around blockchain and cryptocurrency in the public eye, DLT often has more positive connotations when presenting software solutions in a business setting, but the two terms are often used interchangeably, and both of them will be used in this book. A distributed ledger is, quite simply, a record of transactions (like an accounting ledger), which is held simultaneously in several places. This is not the same as multiple users having access to a single database: the strength of a distributed ledger is that there are many identical copies that are all updated with the same transactions as they occur. It means that transactions can be entered to the ledger by any party, and if all the holders of copies agree that the transaction is valid (or strictly speaking reach a consensus), it will be incorporated in every instance of the ledger.

The entries into the ledger rely on cryptography to make the detail of the transactions confidential to the casual observer, and to enable authorized users to check the integrity of the records they hold. Any information to be recorded on the ledger is processed to produce a hash, a unique string of letters and numbers that represents the original content. This cannot be deciphered by anyone who does not have the key to the encryption, in the same way that end-to-end encryption in communication apps such as WhatsApp and secure e-mail systems ensures that only the sender and the recipient can read the content. If you have a record that purports to be identical to the original, then comparing the hash of the information you hold against the hash held in the blockchain provides irrefutable proof that the record you hold is, or is not, genuine.

Here are some of the common terms used to describe the aspects and functions of blockchain and the world of cryptocurrency.

- Records are *decentralized* and administrative functions are *disintermediated*: there is no central agency, for example a bank, making entries into a database under its sole control.
- Transactions posted to the ledger are *immutable*: once they have been validated, you cannot go back and make changes. This is essential to maintain trust in the records.
- The transactions held in the ledger have *positional integrity*. Each block is timestamped and linked to the blocks before and after it.

- The various methods of agreeing transactions to the satisfaction of the whole community are *consensus mechanisms*, of which there are many, some more effective than others.
- Using a consensus mechanism renders the blockchain *trustless*. That doesn't mean that the records cannot be trusted, rather that there is no need to place your trust in any third party.
- A blockchain may be *public, private,* or *permissioned* depending on its structure and degree of decentralization.
- The code within the blockchain that executes transactions is known as a *smart contract*, which is ironic as it is neither a contract, nor particularly smart.
- The ledger is *transparent*: participants can see all the transactions that have been posted. Anyone can access public blockchain records, for instance the Ethereum blockchain can be viewed on Etherscan.io. It is also possible to see the smart contracts that govern transaction behavior. This is important to maintain confidence in the integrity of the recorded transactions but comes with its disadvantages, most notably in the context of commercial confidentiality, which might be compromised by public access. In a permissioned or private blockchain, of course, only those participants to whom access is granted can access the records.
- Participants in a blockchain are *nodes*. They may be *full nodes*, which hold a copy of the entire distributed ledger, or light client nodes, which transact but do not hold all the records.
- Cryptocurrency is the blanket term for digital cash, and noncrypto currencies are known as *fiat currencies*. Strictly speaking, this term refers to those currencies whose value is set by their issuing government (rather than being backed by reserves), but it has become generic in this context.
- Public blockchains and cryptocurrencies should adhere to five core principles: to be open, public, neutral, censorship-resistant, and borderless.

As the picture unfolds other concepts will emerge, but for now, let's start at the very beginning.

Changing Worlds

This is not the first time that a new technology has generated a polarized opinion. In 1995, *Newsweek* published an article about another emerging movement that was taking the world by storm. Writing on "Why the Web Won't Be Nirvana,"[1] Clifford Stoll said: "I'm uneasy about this most trendy and oversold community. …[it] beckons brightly, seductively flashing an icon of knowledge-as-power…" He discounted the "internet hucksters" and their predictions that we would one day be reading books and newspapers over the internet, educating our kids, catalogue shopping online with a point and a click, ordering airline tickets, making restaurant reservations. Could you, quarter of a century ago, have conceived of the ease with which we have come to read, browse, and transact online? Now try to visualize a near future where creators receive enough automatic micropayments for the use of their work to make a good living, where gamers have a viable career as digital asset managers, where you have control of your personal data and can choose who uses it and for what purpose, where you share electricity you generate among your neighbors, and where the provenance of the food you consume and cosmetics you use can be determined with the click of an app on your phone. This is what excites the pioneers in the blockchain and cryptocurrency space and inspires innovators to explore and harness new technologies.

Similar excitement gripped industrialists and investors in the early days of rail travel. The world's first steam railway ran from Stockton on Tees to Darlington in northeast England. Financed by a consortium of industrialists who raised £120,000 for its construction—the equivalent of over $2.5 million today—it opened in 1825 and at full speed ran at a dizzying 15 miles per hour. The steam engine *Locomotion* took two hours to draw 36 wagons of freight and passengers along the eight miles of track. The investors of the 19th century had a vision, but could not have conceived of the rapid change wrought by the expansion of the railways across North America, and today's bullet trains, maglev, hyperloop, or the Channel Tunnel between England and France.

Blockchain is often compared to the internet, not in function but in its potential to disrupt, to deliver unexpected change. In 1989 a very small community of people were using the nascent World Wide Web.

Academics and employees in geographically diverse organizations had for many years used bulletin boards and message systems, often embedded within early ERP software platforms, as a direct alternative to physical, written mail, or telephone calls. It was a difficult medium for the layman to access, something we have forgotten in these heady days of one-click connection, and in this there are direct parallels with blockchain. Mikko Hyponnen of cybersecurity specialists, F-Secure, recalls the complex instructions they had to give to enable people to access their website, carefully explaining the need for internet access (most often achieved by dialing a provider through a modem), a TCP/IP stack, and a browser.[2] Netscape, one of the earliest applications that we would recognize as a modern browser, did not exist and Windows did not have Transmission Control or Internet Protocols built into its software, but for early adopters the new experience was worth the inconvenience.

Just over a decade later, March 2000 saw the bursting of the "dot com bubble" and early speculative internet developments fell by the wayside. Even at that time we could not have imagined the likes of Twitter and its social media peers, nor our eventual reliance on the internet to deliver information to us through video, audio, and community forums. Some science fiction writers over the years came close, including David Brin in his 1990 novel *Earth*,[3] which featured a dynamic global web of information, citizen surveillance, and wireless connections to wearable technology, among other things. We originally used the internet to streamline two-way communication with people we knew and to read brochure websites that replicated the printed word. The things we were accustomed to doing could be achieved more quickly online and there were cost savings to be made. Innovation started out as a linear process before leaping the void to unimagined functionality.

Blockchain is in the same position now. Ten years after the inception of Bitcoin, the first boom-and-bust cycle of cryptocurrency mirrored the dot com journey. Speculative applications all but disappeared from the landscape as the ready money of the early days dried up, leaving the way clear for serious business models with longer term potential. There are still barriers to access and adoption although these are falling rapidly as organizations, notably cryptocurrency exchanges and blockchain game developers, innovate for ease of onboarding and develop applications with a seamless user experience. The main players in the space, I believe, have not yet emerged. And like the pioneers of the internet or the engineers behind the first railways we simply cannot foresee some of the societal and behavioral changes that await us.

The Blockchain Journey

Our journey begins with the launch of the first decentralized digital currency in 2009, something that researchers had been creeping toward for many years. The encryption techniques and the linking chain structure which underpin the Bitcoin blockchain were innovations standing on the shoulders of giants, but the eventual breakthrough published in Satoshi Nakamoto's white paper delivered a new way of working. For the first time, Bitcoin demonstrated the creation and maintenance of a ledger in which transactions could be processed and recorded without the involvement of a central processing agency. It established a system where everyone has a copy of the ledger, everyone agrees that the transactions have been recorded accurately, and no-one can change the records.

Where will this decentralized, transparent, trustless, immutable technology take us, with its complex consensus mechanisms and carefully constructed smart contracts? Blockchain has spawned champions and detractors in equal measure since developers took the first tentative steps beyond decentralized currency. In the years between the publication of the original Bitcoin whitepaper by the pseudonymous Satoshi Nakamoto in 2008, and the launch by Vitalik Buterin's team of the Ethereum Virtual Machine in 2015, blockchain was essentially the preserve of cryptocurrency evangelists and developers. In 2017 this changed as cryptocurrency prices began to rise and mainstream media picked up on the story. The subsequent bull and bear markets attracted attention for their get-rich-quick potential and the schadenfreude of paper losses. Blockchain and crypto have exploded into the public consciousness, but perception varies wildly.

In the minds of some commentators, it is the silver bullet that will come to the rescue when there seems no other way to solve difficult political and business challenges. Others are less convinced. In October 2018, British and American politicians were exposed to both ends of a polarized spectrum. At the British Conservative Party conference, the then Chancellor of the Exchequer, Philip Hammond, was asked about possible solutions for a frictionless land border between the United Kingdom and European Union on the island of Ireland in the event of Brexit.[4] "There is technology becoming available," he replied. "I don't claim to be an expert on it, but the most obvious technology is blockchain." At the same time on the other side of the Atlantic, Professor Nouriel Roubini of Stern Business School testified to the U.S. Senate Committee on Banking, Housing, and Community Affairs: "Crypto is the mother of all scams and (now busted) bubbles, while blockchain is the most over-hyped technology ever, no better than a spreadsheet/database."[5]

Of course, the truth lies somewhere between the two. Roubini's scorn for the scams and bad practice which characterized the early rush for unregulated investment in blockchain projects was valid, but his complete dismissal of cryptocurrency and blockchain ignored the widening adoption of crypto as a valid means of exchange, and the introduction of effective distributed ledger applications to solve genuine problems in multiple sectors worldwide. Hammond's hope for a fast solution to a political impasse came at a time when blockchain was more about unrealized potential, possible use cases, pilot projects and proof of concept than effective, scaled applications. With a tight political deadline looming and an electorate to impress his statement smacked more of desperation than practicality, and according to the BBC's Rory Cellan-Jones, it did not reflect the more practical opinions in the corridors of Whitehall. Blockchain is on course to help with smoothing the passage of goods around the world, but not in the short term, and not in isolation.

Behind the Crypto Headlines

Many people follow the stories about volatile cryptocurrency trading without any appreciation of the hive of activity that surrounds the technology beneath. The rise and fall of cryptocurrency prices and associated scams and snake-oil salesmen make for more lurid headlines. What often goes unreported is that this gold-rush fundraising with new cryptocurrencies (altcoins) and tokens was largely responsible for oiling the wheels of rapid, global, and largely collaborative development. A lot of good work has been going on under the radar to refine and expand upon Bitcoin's original mechanism for decentralized, trustless, transparent transactions. Beneath the hype, there are highly respected professionals developing new ways of working, and a growing number of distributed ledger applications are ticking quietly away under the hood of regular software platforms. Multinational enterprises are putting the structure in place to revolutionize financial technology, supply chain management, utilities, and health care. Individual states, federal bodies, and sovereign nations are establishing legal frameworks for the protection of investors and the use of blockchain in asset registries, identity, and credentialing. The United Nations has a blockchain for social good agenda centered around its multi-UN agency platform,[6] where it invites you to imagine:

> that 2.5 billion unbanked people will be included in the global financial system; that foreign workers will not lose $50 billion collectively per year when sending money to their home across the border;

> that people will know about the life story of a product when they buy it; people who created the product, the places that were involved, the material used etc.;

> that people will live without fear that their land might be appropriated by someone who comes to the door with a gun in their hands;

> that artists will gain autonomy over their copyrighted material and build direct relationships with fans;

> that patients will have control over their personal medical records;

> that foreign aid will reach its intended beneficiaries without losing 30 percent of its entirety.

> that every single person on earth will have an ID and get access to education, health, and other social services.

This is a powerful vision of the kind of future that many advocates believe can be facilitated by evolving blockchain technology.

Legitimacy of Cryptocurrency

The positive outlook of the United Nations is a far cry from the murky reputation that has haunted cryptocurrency in the past as a tool for criminal activity and malpractice. For anyone whose computers have been infected by ransomware which locks their data down and demands payment in Bitcoin, crypto is synonymous with criminality. This was reinforced in the public perception by its extensive use on Silk Road, the dark net marketplace, which was active between 2011 and 2014. Over 9 million Bitcoin transactions were recorded on Silk Road during that time, and toward the end of its operations its escrow accounts were hacked, although much of the lost Bitcoin was recovered. Ironically, Bitcoin itself is an innocent party here. The Bitcoin blockchain is entirely transparent and pseudonymous, not anonymous: every wallet could, in theory and in practice, be linked to a real-world identity, making Bitcoin considerably more traceable than cash.[7] In the case of the 2017 WannaCry ransomware attack, for example, all the ransom payments are visible on the Bitcoin block explorer for anyone to see.

The blockchain tells a story, too. For a high-profile worldwide attack, the fact that only 338 victims in total paid the WannaCry ransom underlines the sterling work of the cybersecurity professionals who stopped the virus in its tracks (thanks in part to quick action by malware researcher Marcus Hutchins[8]) and helped users to repair the damage done by the ransomware without making any payment. Examining the records of one of the three wallets that were used to collect the ransoms, you can see 133 receipts of Bitcoin, which at the time each equated to $300, and the withdrawal of the whole amount in two transactions several months later.[9] The funds were transferred to a wallet in a privacy currency, Monero, where real transaction details are protected by obfuscating the data: six false records are attached to every real transaction, making it harder to follow a trail. This kind of anonymous cryptocurrency is much harder to police, being the digital equivalent of used bank notes. Tarring every digital coin with the same brush is unfair.

Another accusation leveled at cryptocurrency, especially during the rapid price rises of 2017, is that it is a Ponzi scheme, a pyramid, a scam to defraud innocent investors by paying out returns for early adopters from the investments of those late to the party. As the prices have settled back to realistic levels and both volume and regulation have improved there is much less talk of fraudulent practice and a greater understanding of the reliability of mainstream digital currencies. At the time, however, this inaccurate impression was so prevalent that a joke currency "PonziCoin" was created in 2018 by a California developer. The white paper for PonziCoin laid out in clear, unequivocal language that the smart contracts would pay out the first investors from the proceeds of later investments until the money ran out. To the amazement and horror of the team behind the prank, people actually started putting cash into the scheme. They quickly disabled the ability to invest and allowed the smart contracts to run their course. In a statement on their website, the developers gave a warning to people caught up in the hype:[10]

> We hope everyone had a good laugh :) But we have to shut down. This was a parody art performance/joke. I did not "run off" with the money, I never sold any of my PonziCoins, and the contract was drained from other users withdrawing. Please be careful when investing in shady cryptocurrencies, especially ones that look like pyramid schemes—it's a zero-sum game and money doesn't appear out of thin air.

This is a salient lesson for investors in early stage blockchain projects, where tokens can be purchased with such ease. There is a reason why in most jurisdictions investing is regulated to some degree, and if the return from an investment looks too good to be true, then it probably is.

Ultimately, however, cryptocurrency is simply a form of money. Author Yuval Noah Harari writes:[11]

> Money is the only trust system created by humans that can bridge almost any cultural gap, and that does not discriminate on the basis of religion, gender, race, age, or sexual orientation. Thanks to money, even people who don't know each other and don't trust each other can nevertheless cooperate effectively.

Cryptocurrency is the natural evolution of the most universal system of mutual trust ever devised. Its decentralized structure and integral trust mechanisms ensure its legitimate place in society.

Spending Digital Cash in the Real World

Can you spend cryptocurrency? Of course. The physical wallet in my pocket currently contains a visa card, which links directly to a crypto-currency account. I can indirectly pay for coffee and sandwiches with my crypto holdings. The transaction involves an automated conversion to the local fiat currency, as do the cryptocurrency ATMs that already exist to allow withdrawals from crypto accounts to local cash, but it is the frictionless nature of the exchange that is interesting. One state, the tiny Pacific state of the Marshall Islands, has introduced its own local cryptocurrency as legal tender, the Marshall Islands Sovereign. In Venezuela, payment for goods and services from coffee to clothing is increasingly made in Bitcoin, while the government has started insisting on tax dues being settled in their own cryptocurrency, the Petro (you can read more about this in Chapter 3).

Online, I can buy all kinds of goods and services with cryptocurrency. There are several mainstream cryptocurrency checkout tools available, including a standard Blockonomics plugin, which takes payment in Bitcoin on my own WordPress website and deposits the proceeds directly to my crypto wallet without conversion. Blockchain games such as Cryptokitties, Axie Infinity, Neon District, Decentraland, Epic Dragons, EOS Knights, Gods Unchained, and many others can be played with cryptocurrency.

As the volume of users and transactions increase, the volatility of crypto-currencies is likely to settle, reducing the current risk and uncertainty that surrounds them. The rise of stablecoins, a class of cryptocurrency pegged to the value of a real-world asset or currency, may contribute to more rapid adoption as a large part of the risk associated with digital currency is elim-inated. In California, lawmakers introduced a bill in February 2019 to "remit any cannabis excise tax or cannabis cultivation tax amounts due by payment using stablecoins."[12] Facebook's proposed Libra coin introduces another mechanism for adoption. Commentators including Caitlin Long, co-founder of the Wyoming Blockchain Coalition,[13] believe the reach of this powerful global social network will provide citizens of developing nations with access to a store-of-value that is more reliable than their government-backed currencies. The question is not whether we can use cryptocurrency in our daily lives, but how close we are to mainstream adoption.

What's Actually in the Blockchain?

One of the greatest misconceptions about blockchain is that it is a database holding large volumes of immediately legible information, which cannot be tampered with. In reality, it is a database holding strings of encrypted information, and the only reason it cannot be tampered with is that each block has a fixed position in the chain. Changing the data in one block means changing the data in all the blocks that follow it, and that takes more effort to achieve than the benefit that would accrue, if it is possible at all. Each block is remarkably small, and the transaction data that is held on chain is rendered down to a single cryptographic hash, or checksum, of the text, images, or journal entries concerned.

Talk of putting processes "on the blockchain" glosses over these inner workings, but this is entirely normal. How often do people dig under the hood and into the code that delivers the software they use day to day? When you connect to the internet do you think about the functions, protocols, browser technology, and search algorithms, which display your Google results? Do you consider the structure and workings of the World Wide Web, which deliver your seamless communication experience? It's rare. Normally the only question that exercises us is the reliability of our internet connection and the speed with which we can upload pictures of cats. At this early stage of distributed ledger adoption, however, it seems important to review the basic structure of the blockchain. Understanding this can help in decision making when you are judging the suitability of a distributed ledger to solve the problem in hand.

Merkle Trees and Hashed Records

Let's take a Bitcoin blockchain block at random. Block number 575171 was mined on May 8, 2019. Searching for this block reference through blockexplorer.com[14] reveals that there are 2,568 transactions in the block, which holds only 908,496 bytes of data: just under a single megabyte. This compact record is made possible by cryptographic hashing.

A cryptographic hashing algorithm is used to convert an entry of any length into a regular string of letters (upper and lower case) and numbers (0–9). Commonly the algorithm used is a Secure Hash Algorithm 2 (SHA-2) function such as SHA-256 (quite simply, an algorithm that produces a 256-bit, or 32-byte, hash) or SHA-512 (512 bits, or 64 bytes), but there are many other options to produce the unique string required for the confidentiality and integrity of data. The importance of this string is that if the same entry (a document, image, or transaction) is hashed again using the same algorithm, the string will be identical, and the entry's integrity is verified. However, if there has been any change at all, however small, the strings will not match. Even removing a comma from a sentence in this book will generate a different string when the manuscript is processed. A simple application of this comparison might be to prove that a piece of intellectual property has been recorded on the blockchain on a specific date. Hashing the disputed document and verifying that hash against the blockchain can prove that it is, or is not, identical to the original. The first example of blockchain evidence presented in a case in China in June 2018[15] used precisely this technique to prove that an article had been reproduced without permission by the defendants.

In our blockchain, a second round of hashing converts a pair of strings into yet another unique hash, and this process is repeated pair by pair until all the entries have been consolidated into one single string. This hierarchy of hashed strings is a Merkle Tree, and the final string, the Merkle Tree Root, appears in the block. (These are named for Ralph Merkle whose 1979 thesis[16] addressed cryptography in public key systems.) When transactions are verified, as in the Chinese copyright case, it is actually this root that is the subject of comparison. It is quicker to check one root than thousands of strings, and if one change occurs within the strings then the Merkle root would itself change. With me so far? Good.

Closing the Block

We have now compacted all our records down to a single string of letters and numbers. This string sits in a child block at the very end of the blockchain. On the blockchain explorer you can see the reference to its parent, block 575170. Out in the blockchain network computer power is being fired continuously as participating nodes compete to run a new cryptographic hash with a twist. To complete the block, the hash of the contents including an unknown variable must result in a string with a predefined number of leading zeros: The Block Hash. The computer that is first to find a possible variable value to deliver a valid Block Hash is entitled to close the block and open the next one. The calculated variable is the *nonce*, and it is recorded in the block header along with the time-stamp of the solution. This process is known as *mining:* on the Bitcoin blockchain a predefined reward is paid to the successful miner, along with fees for each of the 2,568 transactions in the block.

Immutability

Why do we insist that the blockchain cannot be changed? The answer lies in the structure of the chain, the contents of the block, and the distrib-uted ledger. Our block number 575171 contains a reference to 575170. It will include the Block Hash of 575170 in the calculation of the Block Hash of 575171. If a single party was to attempt to change any transac-tion within 575170, its Block Hash and that of all the subsequent blocks would then no longer match the original details held on multiple copies of the ledger on all the nodes of the blockchain. It is simply too onerous to recalculate the hash of all the subsequent blocks to cover up a change, and someone attempting to do this would never catch up with the pro-gression of the valid chain. The math involved is difficult and time-con-suming, even for the increasingly powerful computer processors used for the purpose. There are valid concerns that the emergence of quantum computing would enable processing powers sufficient to recalculate Block Hashes at a very high speed, but the overarching rule of blockchain secu-rity still applies: the cost of tampering with the records is greater than the benefit that would accrue to any bad actor.

Knowing the structure of a simple blockchain enables you to assess the suitability of the technology for your business challenge more effec-tively. Where verifiable, timestamped, unchangeable records will stream-line processes, cut out costs, improve lives, or reduce risk, then there is a case to consider the use of blockchain. As with every new technology on the horizon, it is not appropriate for speculative re-factoring of existing systems unless there is a genuine requirement for the features it introduces. Industry will not have time, at the current speed of development, to devote resource to the replication of current systems for the sake of it. When word processors replaced typewriters, it took decades to deliver the extra functionality we now take for granted. With the speed at which technology now evolves, we must focus on enhancement.

Where Is Blockchain Taking Us?

Changes wrought by blockchain will be dramatic and disruptive. To take one example, the disintermediation of processes will be a particular challenge for agencies. We have already seen the impact of online booking on travel agents whose business models have moved away from brokerage and toward delivering added value. As decentralized structures move users toward peer-to-peer behavior, agents in more complex sectors such as property sales may find themselves in the same position.

Distributed ledger technology and cryptocurrencies are here to stay. This book will look in detail at cryptocurrencies and the regulation that surrounds them (Chapter 3), business applications of blockchain (Chapter 4), innovations coming from the gaming sector into the mainstream (Chapter 5), and public sector and government adoption of distributed ledgers, including the question of digital identity and ownership of our own data. First, though, let's look back the at the origins of blockchain and the rise of the first decentralized currency, Bitcoin.

CHAPTER 2

The Long Road to Decentralization

The Challenge of a Digital Currency

The weary traveler hoisted a heavy bag over one shoulder and slouched down the ramp into the spaceport. A barrage of unfamiliar sounds and smells assailed their senses, interrupted by the hiss of a disinfectant curtain and the regular sterile tang of CL2. Shaking out a mess of wet feathers in disgust, they looked around for the nearest bar. A new planet? That called for a cocktail.

For decades writers have dropped their characters into alien lands, both on earth and around endless fictional universes, assuming blithely that they have the means and method to settle their bar tab wherever they may be. The fiscal realities of multiple currencies and foreign exchange are rarely essential plot twists. The reader is simply invited to assume that the coins in the traveler's pocket are either legal tender or made of instantly recognizable precious metals, and that galactic credits are accepted everywhere without question. Is there a single overblown interplanetary bank issuing notes and coins of a common currency to the tentacled and furred alike, or is it more attractive to imagine a digital, decentralized currency? Over the many years that galactic heroes have been hanging around in disreputable bars, researchers and cryptographers have been working toward this vision.

Why was it so tricky to achieve? The classic challenges of creating a decentralized currency are the prevention of double spending, the security of funds and the parties involved, and having reliable proof that a transaction has happened. They are closely related. Let's examine a simple movement of money between two individuals. If one person has a dollar bill and hands it to their friend, the original holder can no longer spend that dollar. A physical transfer has taken place. If instead the holder makes a transfer or payment direct from their bank account, the centralized banking system makes an entry in one part of the ledger to indicate money has been withdrawn from the original holder's account, and an equal and opposite entry debits the balance to the recipient's account. The databases held by each of the participating banks show that the transaction has taken place and ownership of the money has changed.

We accept that there is no way to duplicate the physical note at the time of exchange: there is, of course, a constant battle against counterfeit notes and coins that circulate in the real world, but what we are concerned with here is that an exchange of perceived value has taken place. We trust the digital transfer of money because this is subject to the checks and balances of banking, and we can verify transactions on our bank statements. However, if we want to make a transaction using a currency that is not part of a traditional banking system and has no physical form, how is it possible to confirm that the transaction has been completed correctly? Can we be sure that the item of value really has moved out of the first account and into another? After all, it's not hard to duplicate a digital asset. You can make a copy of a document, an image, a file or a folder with a couple of clicks of a mouse and at negligible cost, enabling us to send the same item from one source to many recipients. A digital, decentralized currency must be a neutral and honest ledger, which requires a mechanism to mitigate the risk of fraud, duplication, and counterfeiting. Such a currency also needs to address the creation and supply of money and be accepted as a symbol of value without recourse to traditional physical reserves. Bitcoin, the first real cryptocurrency, met these challenges and succeeded in being the first neutral, open, borderless, public, and censorship-resistant example of digital cash, but the journey was long. Our story begins more than a quarter of a century before the emergence of Bitcoin, when the internet opened up the possibility of collaboration and cooperation between geographically diverse groups who may not have a trust relationship. Reassuringly, it starts with a new problem that requires a novel solution.

Cryptography Leads the Way

The concept and workings of digital cash were first suggested in 1982 by David Chaum in his PhD in Computer Science at UC Berkeley. The title of his thesis,[1] "Computer Systems Established, Maintained and Trusted by

Mutually Suspicious Groups," immediately evokes the trustless multiparty structure of modern distributed ledgers. The proposal of a working system that could be trusted by people who did not trust each other was one of Chaum's key breakthroughs. He also explains, in what is a very well-written and readable paper, that cryptographic techniques will allow data of any nature and volume to be protected while only a single cryptographic mechanism needs to be secured. This distinction between protection and security is important. Chaum calls the secured element a vault: we know it now as a block in our chain, holding the tiny Merkle root of our hashed data. Furthermore, he notes that multiple copies of encrypted data would not compromise security but would enhance survivability: we can compare this to a distributed ledger. The fundamental concepts of the blockchain are all here, but we are still a long way from the eventual solution.

In a contemporary proposal for blind signatures for untraceable payments,[2] Chaum further addressed the confidentiality of transaction information, proof of payment, verification of parties to the transaction, and protection of any stolen payment media (we would think here of credit cards, which were at the time uncommon). He defined the functions, protocol, properties, and auditability of a cryptographically secured blind signature system. Over the following few years, he published multiple papers exploring the mathematical underpinning of virtual currency, and in 1989 founded DigiCash. Thought to be the world's first electronic money system, its Cyberbucks moved between users using the Blind Signature methodology (now commonly known as Chaumian blinding) and the cash was protected in line with all of Chaum's cryptography principles. This digital currency was ahead of its time, launching at the same time as the nascent World Wide Web but well before the internet became established as a consumer tool. There was significant interest in centralized digital money at the time from banks worldwide and from the likes of Microsoft, as this 1994 *Wired* article explains.[3] "The next great leap of the digital age is, quite literally, going to hit you in the wallet. Those dollar bills you fold up and stash away are headed, with inexorable certainty, toward cryptographically sealed digital streams." Centralized banking grasped the concept, to the point that most of our transactions in fiat currency are now effortlessly digital, but DigiCash itself faded away, and there was still a long way to travel toward decentralization.

David Chaum is still active in cryptography: he founded the International Association for Cryptologic Research, the cryptography group at the Center for Mathematics and Computer Science in Amsterdam, the Voting Systems Institute, and the Perspectiva Fund. He is also working on a new cryptocurrency structure, Elixxir, revisiting his original Blind Payment principles.

Cypherpunks and B-money

The 1990s saw the emergence of the Cypherpunk movement. Timothy C. May wrote "The Crypto Anarchist Manifesto" in 1988,[4] an eerie predictor of the "social and economic revolution" that the subsequent development of cryptography and the internet enabled. A community emerged from the Cypherpunk group's mailing list as concerns grew around state control of strong encryption. In the United States, encryption was classed as a munition thanks to its vital role in securing communications during wartime. With the advent of personal computing the technology became commercially necessary, but government restrictions meant that exported software could only use 40-bit encryption to secure its user licenses, something that could be cracked in a matter of days by the average user. The Cypherpunk movement stood up to National Security Agency (NSA) attempts to stifle research and classify patents and succeeded in bringing strong encryption into the public domain. This battle is well documented in Stephen Levy's 2001 book, *Crypto: How the Code Rebels Beat the Government Saving Privacy in the Digital Age.*[5]

On May's 1992 e-mail to the group,[6] reproducing the original manifesto for a new audience, his signature includes word tags that were obscure at the time but are familiar to us today: encryption, digital money, anonymous networks, digital pseudonyms, zero knowledge, reputations, information markets, black markets—and collapse of governments, anticipated in the anarchist vision as a result of the adoption of these technologies and behaviors. It is interesting to reflect that scandals broken through WikiLeaks have had a de-stabilizing influence in just this fashion: Julian Assange, the WikiLeaks founder who also authored the 2012 book *Cypherpunks: Freedom and the Future of the Internet*[7] was a member of the group.

The Cypherpunk community grew throughout the decade and become a major influence on the development of the cryptocurrencies we know today. The group featured extremely high-quality technical discussions alongside the social niceties, distractions, and trolling that arise in every community. The first recipient of a bitcoin transaction, Hal Finney, was a participant, and it is extremely likely that the person or persons unknown behind the Satoshi Nakamoto pseudonym were also Cypherpunks.

Another Cypherpunk community member, computer engineer Wei Dai, published a post in 1998 reflecting on the need for "a medium of exchange (money) and a way to enforce contracts" should centralized governments become obsolete.[8] He suggested solutions for the transfer of money using a distributed ledger; the creation of digital "b-money"; and a process for the effecting of contracts. Wei Dai suggested that transparent transactions should be announced to the whole network to avoid duplication. He described the minting of new coins through the mining process and defined the need and possible structure of smart contracts. These were some of the key missing pieces of the digital cash jigsaw, but another decade passed before a viable cryptocurrency emerged.

During this period the internet went from strength to strength. The emergence of the Second Life platform in 2003 was a testbed for virtual commerce, relying on a native but centralized currency, the Linden Dollar, which could be exchanged for real world cash. Peer-to-peer networks were established for file sharing, notably BitTorrent's protocol, which was launched in in 2005, although the cavalier attitude to music and film copyright displayed by the likes of Napster (1999–2001) and The Pirate Bay (2003 onward) triggered legal action and shutdowns. Twenty-five years after the first steps were taken on the long road to decentralization, technology and the public mindset had finally caught up to the peer-to-peer vision.

Satoshi Nakamoto Versus the Banking Establishment

Although all the pieces of the cryptocurrency jigsaw had been determined in theory through the collective effort of researchers and activists, early electronic cash initiatives such as DigiCash did not gain traction. Among these, possibly the only name we now recognize is that of PayPal, whose vision of electronic cash turned into the development of a highly successful payment mechanism for traditional currencies, but without all the features in place to deliver a truly decentralized and reliable exchange of value.

They say that necessity is the mother of invention, and it took the mother of all centralized disasters to trigger the creation of the first working cryptocurrency, Bitcoin.

On August 9, 2007, BNP Paribas froze three of its funds, revealing that it was unable to value the underlying collateralized debt obligations (CDOs), bundles of subprime loans that had been rolled into the assets of the funds. The loan debts in question had been individually classified according to their level of nonrepayment risk, but then bundled together as collective assets, traded, shuffled, and cut like decks of cards, and bought and sold within the global banking ecosystem. Every transaction further obfuscated the nature of the underlying debts until it became apparent that it was impossible to place a reliable value on the bundles. The valuations upon which the banks had built their castles were not rock, but sand. Just five weeks later, the ironically named Northern Rock, a British bank that specialized in high loan-to-value mortgage lending, found itself unable to offload its subprime bundles to the market. Its request to the UK government for support triggered a run on the bank as savers queued around the block at every downtown branch to withdraw their cash. This was the first high-profile casualty of the torrid 18 months that followed. A year later, the U.S. government bailed out mortgage lenders Fannie Mae and Freddie Mac, but Lehman Brothers, Washington Mutual, and Wachovia filed for bankruptcy. Iceland's three largest commercial banks collapsed, taking the savings of offshore customers with them. The economics editor of the *Guardian* newspaper, Larry Elliott, said with hindsight:[9] "As far as the financial markets are concerned, August 9, 2007 has all the resonance of August 4, 1914. It marks the cut-off point between 'an Edwardian summer' of prosperity and tranquility and the trench warfare of the credit crunch—the failed banks, the petrified markets, the property markets blown to pieces by a shortage of credit." The collapse exposed the high levels of risk in the practices of centralized institutions and our misplaced trust in the banks which played fast and loose with our cash without any transparency. This turbulence provided the perfect conditions for realization of a part of the Cypherpunk vision: circumventing financial institutions when transferring money. As governments worldwide scrambled to plug financial holes, on October 31, 2008 a paper was published under the pseudonym Satoshi Nakamoto. It was entitled "Bitcoin: A Peer-to-Peer Electronic Cash System."[10]

An Elegant Solution

The emergence of Bitcoin was a watershed moment. Satoshi Nakamoto's blockchain proof of concept realized a decades-old vision by finally putting in place a working decentralized mechanism for the prevention of double spending. The jigsaw was complete and a key element, as originally suggested in a 2005 paper by Nick Szabo proposing a concept called "BitGold,"[11] was the inclusion of a timestamp for each transaction. The logic behind this is that if there are attempts to process multiple identical transactions, whether intentionally or coincidentally, then only the first to be timestamped would succeed and be written to the ledger.

The blockchain structure underpinning Bitcoin enabled security and transparency of transactions and incorporates the minting and distribution of coins as each block is created. Some, but not all, of the familiar concepts from the work of cryptographers and Cypherpunks are present in the Bitcoin solution. Wei Dai's suggestion that transactions should be announced to the network for full transparency was adopted. The peer-to-peer network ensures distributed responsibility for the accuracy of the records. The blockchain is a distributed ledger with copies held by multiple nodes, ensuring that no single entity either controls the records or unilaterally confirms the legitimacy of the recorded transactions. The data that is secured in each block is the Merkle tree root, reflecting Chaum's vault, although this was not referenced in the Bitcoin white paper. Digital signatures are an essential part of the solution, but not, in this case, blind signatures. This means that the Bitcoin blockchain is pseudonymous (users could be traced to the real world) rather than anonymous.

Payments of minted rewards and transaction fees are made to the nodes of the blockchain (the cryptocurrency miners) as each block is closed and new one opened. This is the incentive to maintain the system, rather than to defraud it. This cryptoeconomic mechanism is essential to the proper functioning of Bitcoin: it ensures that value derives from resource scarcity, rather than being backed by a scarce physical asset or commodity. As the white paper explains, "The steady addition of a constant of amount of new coins is analogous to gold miners expending resources to add gold to circulation. In our case, it is CPU time and electricity that is expended." When the Bitcoin blockchain was encoded, it included a reserve of 21 million Bitcoin from which rewards are drawn. The early miners claimed 50 Bitcoins for each validation, but the reward halves with every 210,000 blocks. As Bitcoin blocks are timed for creation every ten minutes (although this interval varies in practice), this means that the halving occurs at approximately four-year intervals. To maintain the incentive as rewards fall, miners' earnings will be balanced by increasing transaction fees as the volume of transactions increases. The third halving in 2020 takes the coins in issue to 18,375,000 BTC, although many have already disappeared down the back of the virtual sofa with the inadvertent loss of wallets and hard drives. It will take many more years to distribute the remaining almost three million coins thanks to this system of diminishing rewards.

The 21 million coins created cannot be copied or added to, which allows Bitcoin to function as a store of value. Bitcoin is a genuinely rare commodity in the cryptocurrency space, and as we see other currencies emerging on separate blockchain platforms it becomes clear that each has their own separate function. Bitcoin is the reserve currency for a new class of digital assets and is now frequently listed alongside the dollar and the yen in currency tables. Bitcoin is perhaps closer to the much-vaunted gold standard than fiat currencies: there is no quantitative easing in the world of digital currency.

Far from being an artificial currency, Satoshi Nakamoto ensured Bitcoin could be authentically sustained in the long term. There is constant development and maintenance from the Bitcoin community, and while the currency has certainly evolved, it has functioned reliably for more than a decade.

The first transfer of Bitcoin between two parties took place on January 12, 2009, from Satoshi Nakamoto to Hal Finney. This was almost the last that the community heard of the pseudonymous creator, and the wallet containing mined Bitcoins from the earliest days remains untouched.

Notoriety and Anonymity

Who is Satoshi Nakamoto? There is considerable speculation on the identity of the creator of Bitcoin.[12] The wording of the white paper seems to indicate that "Satoshi Nakamoto" was more than one person, and the influence of the Cypherpunk movement in the construction of the solution suggests that at least one of those people would have been a member of the Cypherpunk mailing list. There has been plenty of effort made to solve the mystery, but most names on the short list of possible candidates have strenuously denied involvement. There is circumstantial evidence that Satoshi was based in Britain or Western Europe. The language of the paper itself is more British or Commonwealth than American, and analysts have determined that no posts were made to the Cypherpunk community by the user between midnight and 6 a.m. GMT. In addition, the curious message hidden in the timestamp code in the first Bitcoin block mined, which reads: "The Times 03/Jan/2009 Chancellor on brink of second bailout for banks," shows the date in British format and references the London newspaper.[13]

Hal Finney, as the recipient of the first Bitcoin transfer, is an unlikely candidate unless it was a deliberately sneaky move to send money to himself. The appropriately named Dorian Prentice Satoshi Nakamoto has been held up by some media outlets as a possible author, but although he lived only a few blocks from Hal Finney in California, there is nothing to link him to either Finney or the Bitcoin project.

Another strong possibility was Nick Szabo, who worked with David Chaum at DigiCash and who, three years prior to the Bitcoin white paper in 2005, wrote about a very similar concept, BitGold. Again, despite circumstantial evidence of similarities between the two, he has denied any involvement.

In Estonia, cryptographers Ahto Buldas, Märt Saarepera, and Mike Gault explored the same system of digital signatures, hashing and time-stamping while working on digital identity in 2007. The timing of their work and its similarity with the Bitcoin solution attracted speculation, but they have not invited attention and like Szabo have denied any involvement.

By contrast, Australian Dr Craig Wright, who worked in partnership with the late David Kleiman in the very early days of Bitcoin, has put himself forward as a pretender to the Satoshi crown. Whether Kleiman or

Wright were involved in writing the white paper and developing the initial code, however, is still unclear. In an interesting twist, Wright applied for and was granted U.S. copyright on both the Bitcoin white paper and the Bitcoin code in May 2019, claiming authorship under the famous pseudonym. As the Copyright Office explained in a press release following these registrations,[14] it does not investigate whether there is a provable connection between the claimant and the pseudonymous author, relying only on the applicant's statement. A complex series of court cases in the summer of 2019, which involved a dispute with Kleiman's estate and, separately, action against people who claimed Wright was not Satoshi, also failed to unearth any evidence supporting Wright's authorship of the paper.[15]

As no irrefutable proof of identity has been brought into the public domain by any of the likely candidates (access to the Satoshi wallet being the most compelling) the crypto community is still divided as to the real identities behind Satoshi Nakamoto. Is this a bad thing? Aside from satisfying our natural human curiosity, most commentators agree it is entirely in the spirit of Cypherpunks and the Crypto Anarchist movement that Satoshi's identity remains unknown. By fading into the background, and therefore not providing a figurehead, the creator(s) of Bitcoin have ensured that the solution remains truly decentralized.

Building on Bitcoin

What kind of transactions can you record in a block? Bitcoin itself works on a form of triple entry bookkeeping where the double entry of sending and receiving a payment is confirmed by a third entry: a digitally signed, cryptographically sealed receipt from the network. Each transaction on the Bitcoin blockchain is processed using a model known as UTXO, or Unspent Transaction Output. Accessing your "wallet" using its public and private keys is actually the process of unlocking the coins to which you are associated. If the keys are mislaid, you cannot open the lock. When initiating a payment, you are unlocking a UTXO and telling the network to take the amount of coins you specify from the total available. The balance, in other words the unspent amount, is sent back to you by the network as a new UTXO, which will be unlocked for the next transaction. It may sound complex, but a user's wallet is really a list of the UTXO records associated with that user, totaled to give an account balance. Every full node on the Bitcoin blockchain holds a copy of all the unspent Bitcoin transactions.

Why should a distributed ledger approach be restricted to financial transactions? The idea of decentralizing processes other than cryptocurrency transactions quickly caught the imagination of developers and enterprises. If you could cut out the middlemen in day-to-day banking, what other agencies could be rendered unnecessary? UTXO is not really a practical methodology for anything other than an exchange of identical digital assets: the idea of writing a second protocol layer on top of the Bitcoin blockchain is credited to J. R. Willett who, in 2012, published "The Second Bitcoin Whitepaper." Crucially for the future of this industry, he also suggested securing development funds to do this from within the crypto community. The original document is no longer accessible, but at the 2013 San Jose Bitcoin conference, Willett explained the idea to his panel's audience.[16] Laura Shin, writing for *Forbes* in 2017, describes the breakthrough.[17] "He dreamed up something like contracts on top of Bitcoin," she explains, "the way e-mail is layered on top of TCP/IP, but wondered how he could pay for its development. [He realized] he could float a coin on top of Bitcoin that buyers would automatically own if they sent bitcoin to fund its development."

Willett succeeded in funding his Mastercoin project through what became known as an Initial Coin Offering (ICO), but the project was not launched on Bitcoin. The Bitcoin blockchain is a robust creature, and by this time its tried and tested structure had been replicated and refined by other blockchains including decentralized name registration database Namecoin (2010), Litecoin, the silver to Bitcoin's gold (2011), and enduring and much-loved joke currency Dogecoin (2013). However, it is not sophisticated enough for the needs of enterprise. Something more tailored was needed to handle additional protocol layers and complex, multistage smart contracts.

Ethereum and the Virtual Machine

In December 2013, Vitalik Buterin published a whitepaper entitled "Ethereum: The Ultimate Smart Contract and Decentralized Application Platform." The Ethereum software itself is open source therefore the whitepaper is a constantly evolving document on GitHub,[18] but the original[19] can be accessed in online archives. Ethereum was the first blockchain infrastructure purpose-built for distributed computing, that is, with the ability to hold multiple protocols above the base cryptocurrency layer. Buterin's vision of smart contracts running autonomous rules to govern the movement of any digital asset went far beyond Bitcoin, and although Ethereum relies on Bitcoin's "credible decentralization" and in particular the timestamping for first-to-file transactions, it reduced blocktime significantly from 10 minutes to around 15 seconds.

The Ethereum Virtual Machine (EVM) enables code to be run within individual nodes, a significant innovation for the development of distributed applications (dApps). Buterin also suggested a logical extension toward "decentralized autonomous organizations (DAOs)—long-term smart contracts that contain the assets and encode the bylaws of an entire organization." The launch of Ethereum was itself part financed by an ICO, which raised the approximate equivalent of $18 million of development funds through the sale of its native currency, Ether (ETH). This opened the floodgates for hundreds of ideas that entrepreneurs believed, rightly or wrongly, would benefit from the unique properties of blockchain.

What are the potential applications of Ethereum? Founder Vitalik Buterin listed his top picks in response to a query from Elon Musk on Twitter in April 2019. The thread included:

> A globally accessible financial system, including payments, store of value, also more advanced stuff like insurance; Identity: "sign in with Facebook" -> "sign in with an Ethereum account, no intermediaries". Also, web of trust...

> All sorts of registries should publish on chain for security and easy verifiability; Experimenting with new forms of human organizational structure; All sorts of micropayment use cases via payment channels; Markets for personal data for privacy preserving machine learning (you pay me X, I let you homomorphically execute function Y on my data that's been attested to by Z ...);

Cryptoeconomics for spam prevention in social networks; Prediction markets for content creation DAOs; Cryptoeconomics / micropayment schemes to reward publishers of good content; Testing ground for new market designs, e.g. frequent batch auctions, combinatorial auctions, automated market makers;

"Peer-to-peer (p2p) marketplace for internet connections / incentivized mesh networks; Identity, reputation and credit systems for those that currently have few resources (e.g., refugees); Decentralized DNS alternatives e.g. Ethereum name service domains."

Some of these applications have already been realized and will be examined in more detail later in this book. Others are tantalizingly out of reach but visible on the horizon of blockchain development. Over time, where the Bitcoin blockchain's native currency began to find its niche as a store of value based upon its programmed scarcity, Ethereum has become the ICO machine. The EVM allows applications built on top of the Ethereum blockchain to operate separately from the host. The decentralized ecosystem that has grown up around this mechanism has developed genuinely new concepts, with open source collaboration yielding new types of token with unique behaviors and properties beyond simple digital cash. The gaming sector in particular has pushed this work forward with ownership of nonmonetary digital assets, of which more in Chapter 5.

Not-So-Smart Contracts and Cautionary Tales

Decentralized contracts were the third feature of Wei Dai's suggestions for b-money. Although the transfer of an asset from A to B is reasonably straightforward, transactions in the wider world can be significantly more complex. Of course, blockchain wasn't the first piece of software to encode business rules, but the need to manage such complex transactions in blockchain applications gave rise to *smart contracts*. This is a terrible name for a piece of code that is neither a contract, nor particularly smart, and causes all kinds of confusion among the uninitiated. Even Vitalik Buterin said in 2018 that he wished he'd called them something quite different. However, smart contracts they became.

The smart contracts that characterize Ethereum's protocol are the rules for a transaction laid out in the ledger's code. There is no contract formed in the legal sense of the word (although the code may be reflective of binding contract conditions), and there is no learning or refinement involved. Our not-so-smart smart contracts have more in common with robotic process automation (RPA) than intelligent machines; they are RPA for mutually suspicious groups.

These snippets of chain code define very clearly a repetitive process to be applied. Movement of cryptocurrency on an account balance basis, rather than the UTXO model, was the starting point, ensuring that transfers from one wallet to another run smoothly without any central intervention. The transaction for a payment is reasonably simple: First, check the details: Is the balance in the originating wallet enough to make the transfer? Is it going to a valid address? What is the appropriate transaction fee? Then the relevant variables are inserted (here they would be originator wallet address, destination wallet address, amount sent, and the fee due) and the resulting transaction reads "send x coins from wallet a to wallet b and send transaction fee y from wallet a to the miner's block reward pot c." This statement is hashed for inclusion in the next available block while the transaction executes and is written to the ledger. If your own record of this exact transaction is checked against the immutable record in the future, the hashed strings will match, and you have verification of its authenticity and the accuracy of your own ledger.

Smart contracts enable transactions to be completed without establishing a relationship with the processor. Instead of putting trust in your bank to process a payment, for instance, you rely on the smart contract in the blockchain of your chosen cryptocurrency to execute the transfer of coin.

Let's think through the kinds of transaction that happen in the real world. In a supply chain, an invoice issued by a supplier must be recorded as a debt in the ledger of the customer but will not be settled until certain conditions are fulfilled. Smart contracts can be used to line up the different elements of authorization such as receipt of goods and confirmation of quality certification among the mutually suspicious groups along the chain, before effecting a transfer of funds from customer to supplier. The similarity to robotic process automation is clear. A smart contract is simply an automated process in a decentralized system. Another example that is commonly quoted as a potential smart contract application is a discharge from hospital treatment, which triggers the creation of a follow-up appointment. This is certainly possible through a distributed ledger, but as it is likely that all the parties to this transaction are known and trusted, then automation within a centralized system is a more appropriate solution.

The significance of smart contracts is their ability to disintermediate any transaction. By removing the role of a central agency, parties can transact directly, even settling their commitments using the platform's native currency. However, there are good reasons to be cautious about disintermediation. If there is an error in a smart contract on which you rely for accurate transaction processing, there is nowhere to go if there is no centralized complaints department. Although a smart contract is not a legally binding contract in itself, there are legal implications to consider. Disintermediated transactions that can be executed across different countries and jurisdictions not only remove the middleman but can also obfuscate the legal and fiscal position of the parties. Although a smart contract is a transactional process and not designed to be contractually watertight, execution may result in the formation of a legally binding contract, either intentionally or inadvertently. Even if a legal contract is the intention of the developer, it may not turn out to be enforceable, and the route to recourse is not clear for the parties under law if there is a dispute. In the case where a legally binding contract is created, and the existence and content of the completed transaction can be authenticated by reference to the immutably stored data, questions arise over what jurisdiction applies, and in the case of borderless cryptocurrency, under what tax system earnings should be declared. This is further complicated by the extraordinary range and diversity of conflicting privacy laws that are in force across the world: which law applies to cross-border interactions and how does the transparency of transactions on a public blockchain play out in different legal systems?

The quality and the usefulness of a blockchain application stands or falls by the quality of the smart contracts encoded within. It is up to developers to ensure that these are effective, efficient, and secure. This code governs the everything from the management of ICO investments to property register updates. The technology is exciting, but there are plenty of potential pitfalls and cautionary tales.

The Price of Gas

Cryptokitties, the first high-profile blockchain game, is a great example of a set of smart contracts managing digital asset transactions (plus, the kitties are cute). The buying and selling of kitties are simple transactions, while breeding kitties involves more complex rules, taking account of the inherited genetic traits of the parents and determining the final makeup of the offspring. The game was an instant hit with the crypto community, so much so that it put considerable pressure on the functioning of the Ethereum blockchain. In so doing, it not only tested the robustness and scalability of the network, exposing concerns that led to greater innovation, but it also opened the eyes of users to the transaction costs beneath smart contracts.

Every smart contract on a public blockchain comes with a cost. This is an inherent part of the Proof of Work consensus mechanism: there must be a reward to miners that makes it worth their while to maintain the blockchain. The reward is made up of coins issued from a reserve, and fees for the execution of each transaction. The transaction fee on the Ethereum blockchain is dependent on the functions in the smart contract and the price of *gas*. Gas is a measure of how much work a particular function takes to perform; it is named for its role as the cryptofuel which drives the motion of smart contracts. Every function has a fee expressed as a number of units of gas, and these are set out in Appendix G of the Ethereum white paper. For example, calculating a single cryptographic hash costs 30 units of gas; an *ADD function to find the sum of two integers costs 3 units of gas; a *COPY operation in a smart contract is charged at 3 units of gas per word. These add up. A payment in ETH, moving the asset from one wallet to another, will cost the transferor in total 21,000 units of gas. When developers are writing smart contracts, there is a new consideration: how gas-efficient is the code? Has the transaction price been minimized for users?

The gas price, in other words the amount of ETH payable per unit of gas, varies according to the volume of transactions being processed.

It is expressed in small denominations of ETH known as Gwei (10^{-9} ETH). A typical price per unit of gas might be 20 Gwei, or 0.00000002 ETH. When Cryptokitties mania was at its height, the gas price was correspondingly high. At the time, using Metamask, the most well-known user interface that allows players to access Cryptokitties and other games, required knowledge of the gas rules. Users were asked what price they would pay for gas, and a range of appropriate values suggested. This was both a barrier to adoption and a learning opportunity, but more recent versions of Metamask and newer wallet interfaces such as Dapper have reduced the complexity for users by automating gas price selection or, in the case of Dapper, absorbing the costs entirely.

The rules of demand and supply meant that in an oversaturated network only those users bidding high for gas had their transactions successfully validated, but crucially, costs are incurred whether or not a transaction succeeds, because processing takes place regardless. Some of my own attempts to breed Cryptokitties at too low a gas price cost me a fraction of an ETH with nothing to show for it. That's a trivial loss, but something you don't want your users or your investors to experience.

The Cost of Getting Things Wrong

The most notorious transaction fee disaster to date occurred when an overeager investor fell afoul of a smart contract error during the ICO for AirSwap in October 2017. Attempting to buy 1,700 ETH worth of tokens, the investor set the transaction gas price ridiculously high at 400,000 Gwei (0.0004 ETH) per unit of gas, possibly to ensure that their transaction had top priority for validation. Unfortunately, the smart contract had been set up with a gap in the sale window. The transaction arrived on the network at a time when the contract was unable to transfer tokens to the buyer and the resulting error automatically invalidated the attempted purchase. The investment ETH was not transferred, but just short of 237 ETH in transaction fees were charged, the equivalent of over $70,000 at the time. At normal gas prices, the 592,379 units of gas should have cost the transferor around $3.50.

This cautionary tale should prompt developers to get things right at launch, but smart contract development issues prevail. These are not only a concern in structuring contracts correctly, but also ensuring that they are secure in the face of cyber threats. Hartej Sawhney, cofounder of blockchain and smart contract security specialists Hosho Group, gave me a clear picture of the current state of play.

> "The quality of smart contracts being written in the industry is slowly but surely improving," he said. In 2017 and 2018, it was not uncommon to discover critical vulnerabilities such as "infinite token generation" inside smart contracts. Companies were proudly copying and pasting large chunks of other companies' smart contracts and praying that the code would compile and do what functions they intended.
>
> There has been a lack of incentive for talented individuals in InfoSec to learn blockchain languages such as Solidity and to provide security services in the space. Standard practices for security such as those found in the United States financial industry could do much good to the Blockchain industry. Most companies lack the sophistication to ensure security is given priority [and] that regular penetration testing and auditing is conducted.

This is a real concern, and also an opportunity for companies like Hosho. Developers have an ethical responsibility to collaborate and support each other to deploy effective and secure smart contracts throughout blockchain applications, and business leaders must be aware of the standards that must be upheld to protect users and the business itself.

Hacks, Forks, and Infighting

Cryptocurrency has not been without controversy. The original Bitcoin blockchain's code, released under an open source license for the use of all, has spawned clones and competitors over the years. While imitation may be the sincerest form of flattery, some of the new currencies have a murkier history rooted in errors, attacks, and bitter differences of opinion. It is normal for changes to be made to public blockchain code. The open source community takes responsibility for maintaining and updating chains, improving security, speed, and capacity as demand for transaction recording grows and relevant technology improves. When a change is agreed by community consensus, this results in a *fork* of the blockchain in question, pausing activity and implementing new code before moving forward, hopefully more efficient but to all intents and purposes unchanged. If the new code is backward compatible with the existing software, this is a *soft fork*. In cases where the new code is more disruptive, we have a *hard fork* in the chain, which requires all nodes to update to the new protocols before continuing block confirmations.

The complication arises where developer communities find themselves irreconcilably divided over the best course of action for the existing chain. This results in a *contentious hard fork*. There are good examples of contentious hard forks on the Bitcoin blockchain (the Bitcoin Cash saga) and on the Ethereum blockchain (The DAO Hack). Let's have a look at how these arose.

Changing Direction: Bitcoin Cash

In 2017, Bitcoin developers spent considerable time addressing the shortcomings of the original blockchain protocol that had been exposed through almost a decade of advancing technology and greater demand for transaction throughput. As the chain grew longer the throughput of transactions recorded in each tiny 1 Mb block slowed, causing frustration and increasing costs as people paid premiums for faster validation. There were several solutions proposed by the community with the aims of reducing the data recorded and / or increasing the size of the block. One proposal known as Segregated Witness (SegWit) changed the order of processing for block confirmation, segregating elements of a transaction to reduce the volume of recorded data and thereby speed up processing. A second phase of Segregated Witness (SegWit2x) aimed to increase the block size from 1 Mb to 8 Mb. In the end, the Bitcoin blockchain only adopted the first phase of SegWit through a soft fork. Most of the community backed down from making a hard fork implementation of larger block sizes, but a minority of objectors decided to go ahead and create a new fork of the Bitcoin blockchain, called Bitcoin Cash. This came into being on August 1, 2017. Other forks to create different currencies with different mining structures, notably Bitcoin Gold and Bitcoin Diamond, also occurred in 2017.

The Bitcoin Cash story does not stop here. The new currency gained traction, while the core Bitcoin blockchain continued on its way with 1 Mb blocks. Bitcoin Cash was widely promoted as the cryptocurrency that Bitcoin should be, and a roadmap for its development was laid out. However, a year later the two key developers involved in Bitcoin Cash, Roger Ver and Craig Wright, disagreed over the direction that the currency was taking. A planned soft fork of Bitcoin Cash took place in November 2018, moving the roadmap forward under the leadership of Ver. Wright and his team took a different path and hard forked to create a new chain, which they claim reinstated the original Bitcoin protocols from 2009, known as Bitcoin Cash: Satoshi's Vision.

Confused? This is normal. The philosophical differences that arise between Bitcoin developers in a quest to achieve the perfect peer-to-peer system of electronic cash may haunt us for years to come.

Computer Says Yes: The DAO

Ethereum is not prone to as much infighting as Bitcoin, possibly because the developer community includes founder Vitalik Buterin rather than being distracted, as Bitcoin is, by speculation over the identity of Satoshi. This does not mean that contentious forks don't happen, and the forking of the Ethereum blockchain to create a second currency, Ethereum Classic, came about following an attack on an application known as The DAO. This hack in June 2016 was the daddy of all smart contract disasters.

In his original 2013 white paper, Vitalik Buterin noted in relation to smart contracts that, "[the] logical extension ... is decentralized autonomous organizations (DAOs)—long-term smart contracts that contain the assets and encode the bylaws of an entire organization." In 2016, a team of developers launched The DAO, an investor-directed venture capital fund whose structure was a realization of Buterin's original idea. Funds contributed by investors would be distributed automatically to ventures selected by the system and approved by consensus, and the returns would be shared among the members, with all the transactions governed by smart contracts and untouched by human (centralized) hand. A successful

ICO was launched, and the team sat back and watched the money roll in from more than 18,000 investors. Sadly, there were underlying flaws in the smart contracts governing the approval of suitable ventures and the distribution of investment funds. A hacker succeeded in manipulating the contracts to send around $50 million of the funds, a third of the total, to themselves. The horrified DAO team could only watch as their own smart contract carefully executed immutable transactions in favor of the hacker and the money rolled straight back out again. They could do nothing to stop the code running, and the transactions were irreversible.

In this case, the Ethereum community controversially reached a consensus to roll back the blockchain to a point before the ICO. Later entries on the Ethereum distributed ledger ceased to be valid, and the next transactions to be processed were recorded in a new block referencing as its previous neighbor a block prior to the hack. Not all of the community was comfortable with this action. It went against the principle of immutability to change anything that had gone before. The dissenting minority did not implement the fork and thereby created a second blockchain, Ethereum Classic: This chain still incorporates the DAO transactions.

The whole DAO affair was the final straw for the U.S. Securities and Exchange Commission (SEC). Their report on the hack determined that the tokens offered for sale were securities under the Securities Act of 1933 and therefore should be regulated as such. This started the process for development of strict regulation for the conduct of ICOs and the protection of investors, and arguably slowed down blockchain innovation in the United States as entrepreneurs sought more sympathetic jurisdictions for ICO fundraising.

Challenges of Expanding to Enterprise

The underlying technology of blockchain caught the attention of enterprise very quickly, and it became clear that there was potential to use distributed ledger technology to good effect in multiple industry sectors. However, the volatility of cryptocurrencies, the public nature of the existing blockchains, and the SEC movement toward securities regulation after The DAO was not an ideal environment for the development of commercially sensitive technology. Enterprises needed some way to harness blockchain. The rewards to be reaped from a trustless commercial net-work, for instance in the context of a supply chain, could be to reduce the administrative burden of repeated checks as raw materials move through iterations of processing, or products pass through borders, or to provide verifiable proof of compliance with regulation through an immutable record. This functionality could be achieved with an application built on top of Ethereum, but the transparency that characterizes blockchain is not something always welcomed by businesses. How could a network of mutually suspicious organizations keep their distributed ledger out of the public domain and thereby protect commercially sensitive information?

Permissioned Blockchains

To solve the problems of privacy and verification, a variant of distrib-uted ledger technology has emerged: the permissioned blockchain. These are intended to replicate all the benefits of blockchain as a transparent, immutable record, but eliminate the anonymity of users and open view-ing of transactions and smart contracts, which are features of public blockchains. A permissioned blockchain restricts participation to those parties who have the credentials to access the data on the ledger. These permissions may even be granular within the platform, allowing some parties to submit transactions, and others to view a limited part of the whole record on a need-to-know basis. Many of the case studies later in this book involved permissioned systems.

It is possible to create a private Ethereum blockchain. These are most often used as a testing environment for applications that will eventually move into the public arena, but there are some notable private Ethereum innovations running at scale. These include the World Food Programme's Building Blocks project,[20] which uses a version of Ethereum developed by Parity Technologies.

The Hyperledger Project

Work on permissioned frameworks has been pushed forward by the Hyperledger Project. This started out as a collaboration between the Linux Foundation's open source community and commercial giants including

IBM, Hitachi, Intel, Soramitsu, and Huawei, and in 2019 Microsoft, Salesforce, and Consensys joined the consortium. Hyperledger's growing suite of open source tools includes several frameworks with specific use cases and a number of auxiliary software modules. Frameworks released to date include: Iroha (with Hitachi) for infrastructure projects; Sawtooth Lake (with Intel) for supply chain and provenance, particularly using sensors as a source of prime entry; Fabric (the foundation of the IBM Blockchain platform) for supply chain featuring channels for private and commercially sensitive transactions; and Indy (with Sovrin Foundation), purpose-built for distributed identity.

Distributed Ledger Frameworks

The requirements of specific industries have given rise to several distributed ledger frameworks, which have diverged from the traditional blockchain structure. These include the R3 Corda framework, which is commonly adopted in financial services. Here we could also include IOTA's Tangle, which is designed to handle the ever-widening landscape of the Internet of Things and specialist cross-border payment systems such as Ripple and Stellar Lumens, although these differ from other permissioned systems in that they make use of a native cryptocurrency.

The large R3 Corda consortium includes banks from across the world and has developed a number of private, notarized frameworks in-house and with partners for applications including interbank settlements, trade finance, letters of credit, and securities. Corda's structure is interesting as it requires a centralized notary function as the glue that holds together the decentralized community of participating enterprises. This role is examined in more detail in the Insurwave case study in Chapter 4.

Reaching Consensus Without Coins

A permissioned distributed ledger such as Hyperledger or Corda takes from Bitcoin and Ethereum the highly effective and stable first-to-file timestamping of transactions and the ability to create smart contracts to govern business processes but has no cryptocurrency element. At a fundamental and practical level, how can a private distributed ledger run as a trusted record keeping vault without a Proof of Work system, a native cryptocurrency paying miners to maintain the blockchain and act as a mechanism to randomize confirmations? If there are no monetary incentives for participants to compute the nonce value required to close one block and open a new one, how can the integrity of the blockchain and the records secured within it be guaranteed? Let's look in more detail at the cryptoeconomics within blockchain and the mechanisms that maintain the integrity of the ledger.

Consensus Mechanisms and Cryptoeconomics

Research into the development of new Proofs, or consensus mechanisms, is not only important for the operation of distributed ledgers without cryptocurrency, but for the wider operation of blockchain going forward. As concerns grow over the environmental impact of all the computing power deployed in maintaining these decentralized networks, there is a need to investigate all possible avenues. The environmental and sustainability aspect is covered in greater detail in Chapter 7; for now, let's review the operation of consensus mechanisms and the different ways in which they are implemented for public and permissioned blockchains.

Transaction details for inclusion in a block are recursively hashed to a single string of letters and numbers, the Merkle Tree root of all the data. This string sits in a child block at the very end of the blockchain, along with a reference to the previous block. Closing the block and opening the next one is an essential operation, which, for the integrity of the chain, cannot be centralized or left to specific nodes, and must be sufficiently robust that the nodes of the chain agree, in other words reach a consensus, that the operation is valid and complete. This ensures that data is consistent across nodes and prevents malicious manipulation.

The Role of a Consensus Mechanism

The problem that a consensus mechanism tries to solve is this: In a network of mutually suspicious parties there should be a way to agree on the current state of the ledger. Work on consensus fault tolerance in software goes back to the late 1970s, and a paper describing "The Byzantine

Generals Problem" was published in 1982.[21] This describes the challenge for fictional army generals reaching consensus on the optimal joint attack strategy without direct communication or established trust. Achieving Practical Byzantine Fault Tolerance (PBFT), a complex mathematical construct, is the aim of the algorithms that underpin the various consensus mechanisms in use. There are broadly three ways to approach the problem: by lottery, voting, or work.

Proof of Work

The original Bitcoin blockchain consensus mechanism is Proof of Work (PoW), the work being the computational effort of the miners. It is not simply a consensus mechanism but is intrinsic to the cryptoeconomics of the currency: it is the method by which new coins are brought into circulation. This competitive proof derives from an earlier concept called HashCash.[22] The computation for each block is hard to solve, taking considerable processing power, but easy to verify once completed. The miners are calculating possible *nonce* values for a given value of N in the equation "hash(blockcontents + *nonce*) = a string with N leading zeros." You can see the winning nonce value and the resulting hash of the block with its leading zeros on every block via a block explorer. The first miner to solve the equation earns all the transaction fees and a reward from the diminishing reserve of Bitcoin. This is a proof that has stood the test of time and has been implemented in around three quarters of cryptocurrencies by market capitalization, according to figures tracked by Cryptoslate.[23]

Proof of Stake

In Proof of Stake (PoS), the miner's investment is in their stake in the system, not in computation power. Miners earn fees for the transactions that they validate, and then nodes must majority vote to commit the operation and close the block. The higher your stake, the more transactions you will validate. There are some concerns that bad actors could achieve domination of the consensus through building their stake or a consortium of stakes beyond 51 percent, giving them majority control and the ability to validate and commit fraudulent or duplicate transactions.

A variant of Proof of Stake, Delegated PoS (DPoS) uses real-time voting combined with a measure of the voter's reputation. Token holders nominate a delegate to vote on their behalf, and these delegates earn fees from the transactions in the blocks they sign.

PoS requires miners to stake their coins for the chance to commit (*forge*) the next block in the chain, and the system chooses one of the participating nodes either at random or by selecting the node that has the longest interval since last forging a block (coin age randomization). In case of cheating, for example, validating a fraudulent transaction, the stake is forfeit, which incentivizes honesty. The costs of participation are lower, as there is no algorithm processing to consume energy, and this encourages greater participation in the consensus, which contributes to effective decentralization. It sounds simple but there are many challenges to overcome to maintain the integrity of a single unbroken chain. In particular, developers recognize that there is an opportunity for competing chains to occur by accident or design, or for early participating nodes to seize control and invalidate later transactions. The technical detail behind this is complex; for further reading, there are a number of excellent articles online that explain this in more detail. Different chains have developed different methods of ensuring that miners maintain the right chain at all times, but none have quite succeeded in replicating the incentive in Proof of Work, whereby the cost of equipment and energy that would be expended in attempting to divert the chain are simply too great for miners to attempt such a coup.

NXT is one of several blockchains that uses a PoS consensus, and Ethereum's community has invested a lot of work in developing its Casper update in anticipation of an eventual move from Proof of Work to Proof of Stake.

There are several variations on the Proof of Stake consensus, which, again, require no energy to be consumed in computational intensity. Principal among these are Delegated Proof of Stake (DPoS) and Proof of Authority (PoA). DPoS is equally energy efficient and relies upon a network of witnesses delegating validation duties to a small community of nodes. Notable DPoS blockchains include EOS, BitShares, Steem, and Lisk. Proponents argue that this is a more democratic system than PoS, but the small number of delegated nodes causes concern over centralization: for example, EOS has only 21 delegated nodes, although there are tens of thousands of witnesses. PoA has a similar structure, with a small number of preapproved validators who are staking their reputation on maintenance of the chain. As time goes on, this may prove to be the more powerful incentive. PoA has been cautiously adopted by some of the more centralized blockchains including Ripple.

Lottery and Voting

For an enterprise blockchain, nodes are invited to the network. There is no public aspect, no cryptocurrency, therefore no monetary incentive in the form of transaction fees or mining rewards. It is impractical to use a Proof of Work model, so developers must turn to lottery or voting mechanisms instead.

The Paxos protocol has been the foundation of much of the development of consensus mechanisms, but the landscape is diverging and evolving. Hyperledger and Intel's Sawtooth Lake framework uses Proof of Elapsed Time (PoET). This is a lottery consensus where the network pings the Intel chips in every active node to see which has the shortest wait time for processing (stochastic selection). This node is elected the leader and creates the next block in the chain. Other Hyperledger frameworks have turned to voting, for example, Yet Another Consensus (YAC), ordering services such as Kafka, or to a Simplified Byzantine Fault Tolerance (SBFT) model thanks to the fact that in a private distributed ledger the peers are all known. The Raft consensus mechanism, rolled out to Hyperledger users in 2019, was developed in an effort to produce an understandable consensus mechanism,[24] separating the key elements of consensus and providing a good foundation for system building and education.

As more public and private blockchains are developed, adoption increases, and understanding of cryptography improves further we can expect to see more specialized consensus mechanisms and common standards emerging.

The explosion of cryptocurrency and the development of blockchain applications excited entrepreneurs and put regulators on high alert. Let's see how this complex relationship plays out in Chapter 3.

CHAPTER 3

Magic Internet Money

Money doesn't grow on trees, but the Initial Coin Offering (ICO) crowd-funding method inspired by J.R. Willett resulted in cryptocurrencies sprouting everywhere. This new way of raising money attracted attention from well-intentioned entrepreneurs and snake oil salesmen alike. Here was a pot of unregulated, magic money created from thin air by the issuance of *tokens* native to the application, some floating on top of Ethereum and others generated in completely new blockchains. A growing interest in cryptocurrency from the wider community meant that crowdfunding in this way for blockchain projects caught the imagination of people with money to spend in pursuit of the next big tech success.

Some of these projects have been genuinely innovative, based on good business sense and responding to a real-world problem by proposing an appropriate solution. Certain among them knuckled down to developing the technology stacks that would enable use of distributed ledger in the long term, putting in place the protocols and tools for future development. Others went straight for consumer adoption with varying degrees of success. Notable early ICOs that continue to deliver on their original vision included Ethereum, IOTA, NXT,[1] and Augur.[2] Three of these deal with the infrastructure that is needed for wider use and easy adoption of blockchain: Ethereum with its smart contracts and Virtual Machine, IOTA with its evolving cryptography and scalable Internet of Things transactions through the Tangle verification mechanism, and NXT publishing an open-source blockchain for financial and public services, using Proof of Stake consensus. The Augur project is user-facing: a peer-to-peer oracle and prediction market protocol where users are financially rewarded for correctly forecasting the outcomes of future events.

Some excellent concepts and innovations have emerged around blockchain's new way of solving old problems. As venture capitalists Alyse Killeen, Gil Beyda, and Jimmy Song explained at Austin's SXSW festival in March 2019,[3] people are revisiting business models that did not work on earlier technology, and as long as the problem to be solved is clear before jumping into developing a solution (a common trap in software) there are serious propositions that are attracting traditional support from reputable investors alongside ICO funding.

Gold Rush Scams and Broken Business

Unfortunately, most projects that proliferated at the early stage were not such good business prospects. Research by Statis Group[4] determined that almost 80 percent of the ICOs launched in 2017 were scams, according to findings based primarily on projects failing and founders disappearing once funds were raised. Poor quality white papers behind glossy websites, and fraudulent claims of association with high-profile advisors, drew in the unwary in search of a quick buck. The wider market homed in on blockchain startups with an unerring instinct for shaky high potential ideas, and investors looking for a chance to get rich quick jumped in. Reassuringly, it seems that the Pareto principle applies to investment in ICOs as it does in so many areas of business. Statis noted that "over 70 percent of ICO funding (by $ volume) to-date went to higher quality projects." The discerning investor triumphs, but there have been casualties along the way. Not everyone subscribes to the adage that if it looks too good to be true, it probably is, and legislation to protect the unwary has been running to keep up.

The new gold rush gave Bitcoin and blockchain a bad name. The question is, did cryptocurrency break the system, or was the system broken before?

According to journalist and author Dan Lyons, there are some dubious practices that have their roots far back in management science. His 2018 book *Lab Rats*[5] tells a century-long tale of organizational priorities shifting from the benefit of workers to the benefit of shareholders, normally the founders and principal funding providers. Companies became more focused on delivering returns to their investors, and pressure to perform meant that these returns were not necessarily related to profitable and sustainable business models. Pension funds were raided to prop up share prices in long-established enterprises. Disruption of the workplace, sacrificing long-term employment for the sake of short-term productivity, increased staff turnover. We are now moving inexorably toward what is positively described as the "gig economy," a benefit for shareholders but not for those workers whose income is gradually being eroded and employment rights compromised. In the end, says Lyons, many investors in Silicon Valley and beyond settled on a profitable business model of "grow fast, lose money, go public, cash out," taking quick returns at exit and jumping the traditional, messy, long-winded stage of building a working, profitable business. Speaking to Lyons, he points out that this has all the hallmarks of a classic Ponzi scheme, with public investors paying out the early round shareholders and more often than not watching the share price decline thereafter.

If investors rewarded loss-making enterprises by putting up several rounds of funding in the search for the next Facebook, how did this change the behavior of entrepreneurs? An expectation grew that a good idea was enough to justify financial support. The system was already broken: throwing cryptocurrency into the mix made a lethal cocktail.

When Lambo, When Moon?

As cryptocurrency prices rose rapidly in the latter half of 2017 the craze for the Next Big Thing reached its peak. At the time, many crypto enthusiasts were confident that the market was adjusting to put Bitcoin in its rightful place, sweeping all other coins and tokens along for the ride. "To the moon!" was the cry, or if not moon, then would crypto deliver a Lamborghini? Many early adopters of Bitcoin took sizable profits from the bull market, and it is good to see that they continue to champion cryptocurrency and blockchain development by investing their coins in new enterprises, notably in the gaming sector, which is examined in greater detail in Chapter 5. There is a significant downside, though: not everyone was a winner. Newcomers who bought in at the peak of the 2017 bubble, before prices dropped back down to a more sustainable level, were disillusioned and angry. Accusations flew that this was the real Ponzi scheme, sucking in new investors to reward the existing crypto holders and leaving late arrivals with worthless assets. Price volatility and suspicions of manipulation through repeated Tether exchange transactions[6] (buying and selling Bitcoin through a cryptocurrency pegged to the U.S. dollar to drive price and volume) added fuel to the fire of opponents and skeptics. Warren Buffett called Bitcoin "a delusion" in an interview with CNBC in 2019,[7] although the veteran investor apparently has a more positive view of the underlying distributed ledger technology. In October 2018, Professor Nouriel Roubini of Stern Business School testified to the U.S. Senate Committee on Banking, Housing, and Community Affairs.[8] He titled his talk "Crypto is the mother of all scams and (now busted) bubbles, while blockchain is the most overhyped technology ever, no better than a spreadsheet/database."

The backlash against this period of extreme volatility was understandable. Crypto and blockchain supporters doubled down, and *HODL* became the watchword (this stemmed from an overexcited and misspelled tweet, which had intended to urge people to *hold* their cryptocurrency). The Lambos seemed far away, the moon doubly so. But every cloud has a silver lining, and this turbulent time was no exception. Not only did it clean out many of the speculative and foundationless projects, which only had their eyes on magic internet money, but it accelerated legislation in multiple jurisdictions to protect investors and put blockchain project crowdfunding on a firm footing.

Taming the Wild West of Token Fundraising

New ideas are proposed daily by entrepreneurs who are attempting to raise funding through the mechanism of token sales to the community. The best of these are transformational, the worst unfeasible or fraudulent, but the rapid development of blockchain applications owes much to the easy availability of capital. Where the proposals are sound, and the project is backed by a competent and effective team this advances our understanding of the technology and its potential. However, if a new enterprise is not sufficiently robust to attract the attention of traditional investors such as venture capitalists and banks, or to succeed in mainstream crowdfunding, this is a signal to be wary. A token sale can collect significant investment without the project having been rigorously or independently reviewed. There are good reasons for the existing share issue legislation around the world, which protects uneducated investors from putting their money into something they do not understand. It is inevitable that all jurisdictions are seeking to extend existing regulation and implement new rules for token fundraising to protect investors from themselves.

Utility Versus Security

An important distinction has emerged around the function of the token being offered for sale. In many jurisdictions the regulations imposed depend upon whether the token has a utility in the blockchain project under scrutiny. If there is no utility, then the offer for sale of tokens is likely to involve the investor taking on board a degree of risk and certain rights and obligations that are comparable with the purchase of shares and securities. Of course, the issuance of debt and equity for business funding is heavily regulated in all jurisdictions, and the idea of circumventing the paperwork by simply shoehorning a token into the business plan is strangely attractive to some founders. I work with businesses who are considering or are already using emerging technologies, and unfortunately this is a common theme. Can we put this "on the blockchain" and build in a token? In the vast majority of cases the answer is no, and some approaches have bordered on the downright irresponsible, aiming to pass the whole burden of risk on to speculative token holders like a digital lottery ticket.

What is a utility token? As tokens are programmable, they can have a specific role in the operation of the application. You could consider a pre-sold token as a gift card: buy it now, use it when the system is built. In the case of Ethereum, for example, the native token Ether (ETH) has utility in the settlement of transaction fees and payment of rewards to miners in the Proof of Work consensus mechanism. The Ethereum blockchain could not function without it because the network itself is decentralized, and users must have ETH in order to transact. This utility status from the point of view of U.S. legislators was confirmed by Bill Hinman, Director of Division of Corporation Finance at the Securities and Exchange Commission, in June 2018[9] when he said,

> based on my understanding of the present state of Ether, the Ethereum network and its decentralized structure, current offers

and sales of Ether are not securities transactions. And, as with Bitcoin, applying the disclosure regime of the federal securities laws to current transactions in Ether would seem to add little value.

Another common analogy that may be easier to envision is a business selling advance tickets for the rollercoaster at a discount, with the proceeds of sale invested in building the theme park. Is this ticket a utility, because it allows you to ride the rollercoaster, or a security, because you have helped to fund the capital expenditure on the construction of the park and have an expectation of a return? In this case it is a utility, because the return is not participation in the success of the park but the opportunity to use it. If the park doesn't get built for any reason, then the token holders have no benefit. If the enterprise that raised the funds has not, for example, held funds in escrow pending investment in the development, then there is no recourse. This is why investors in tokens must exercise caution and ensure that they have all the detail with which to make an informed decision.

The position of different jurisdictions on the utility versus security spectrum differs considerably: as a rule of thumb the United States is heavily risk-averse while mainland Europe is considerably more relaxed. The United Kingdom sits neatly between these extremes, and territories including Malta, Gibraltar, and the Swiss canton of Zug have developed legislation that is attractive to enterprises in the field of blockchain and cryptocurrency. Regardless, the sentiment that utility and security are important distinctions is shared. The difference of approach is more reflective of the existing structure of legal systems and constitutions, the state's treatment of similar real-world assets and structures, and the degree to which each legal system is codified. These all vary enormously. Note that, although the specific legislation referred to in the following paragraphs will be superseded in time, the underlying approach of each country is probably too deep rooted to change markedly.

United States

The different layers of legislature in the United States and the tradition of codification, which accompanies a written constitution, have historically contributed to a patchwork of laws at state and federal level that can conflict with each other. The nascent legislation around blockchain and cryptocurrency is no different. Leading the field is the state of Wyoming, whose legislature had passed 13 new laws by early 2019 supporting and framing a welcoming environment for blockchain and cryptocurrency innovation. As Wall Street veteran and Wyoming Blockchain Task Force member Caitlin Long explains, this "[enables] innovation and creativity … to bring capital, jobs and revenue into Wyoming." Covering key aspects of digital asset ownership, custodianship to bring crypto businesses in line with federal legislation, and support for fintech innovators, the Wyoming laws are gradually being adopted by other states. They have paid attention to the U.S. tendency to class tokens as securities rather than utilities and modeled their legislation accordingly to deal with native blockchain securities in line with the treatment of any traditional security.

In April 2019, the SEC issued its Framework for "Investment Contract" Analysis of Digital Assets.[10] Intended as "an analytical tool to help market participants assess whether the federal securities laws apply to the offer, sale, or resale of a particular digital asset," the statement, signed by Bill Hinman and Valerie Szczepanik, senior advisor for Digital Assets and Innovation, clarified that the majority of digital asset sales are likely to be treated as securities. Hard on the heels of this guidance, the SEC sent its first No Action Letter to new venture Turnkey Jet for issuance of utility tokens. There were strings like steel hawsers attached to Turnkey Jet's token sale, including requirements that the funds could not be used to develop any part of the software platform, and that the token must have immediate usefulness within the application. Reaction to the SEC Framework and No Action Letter was mixed, and many observers were disappointed in what is seen as a continued overly restrictive stance. Joshua Ashley Klayman, U.S. Head of FinTech and Head of Blockchain and Digital Assets at Linklaters LLP, was philosophical. Speaking to Modern Consensus when the Framework was released, she said:

> The SEC has been saying for a long time that nearly every sale of digital assets is going to be the sale of a security. Why people keep expecting a different answer from them, I don't know. I think if we want a different result, we need to look to lawmakers.

The lawmakers were ready. Before the ink had dried on the SEC's Token Guidance, U.S. federal legislators introduced two bills supporting the blockchain industry: The Token Taxonomy Act of 2019 and the Digital Taxonomy Act. Writing in *Forbes*,[11] Klayman reflects "how remarkable and powerful it is to have broad bi-partisan support for non-security token sales." As in Wyoming the primary driver for these bills seems to be concern over a lack of regulatory clarity, which Congress believes has stifled innovation and sent businesses overseas to more welcoming jurisdiction. The bills have been drafted with feedback from the blockchain industry, but there are still concerns, including from Wyoming itself where Caitlin Long notes that there are conflicts between the Token Taxonomy Act and some of the legislation that has already been enacted over several states. U.S. efforts continue to codify blockchain and cryptocurrency legislation consistently at state and federal level in a way that eliminates ambiguity, but satisfying all parties is going to be a challenge.

United Kingdom

The Financial Conduct Authority (FCA) in the United Kingdom has a simpler task because it is working within a very different legal framework. UK law is not excessively codified. It relies upon principles and precedent, and there is no desire to overcomplicate blockchain and cryptocurrency regulation. The FCA's guidance[12] categorizes cryptoassets according to their structure and their designed use. Exchange tokens, in other words cryptocurrencies that are essential to the operation of a decentralized platform such as Ether, Bitcoin, IOTA, and XRP, are outside the scope of FCA regulation, as are utility tokens, which provide access to a product or service on a decentralized platform. Security tokens are identified as such if they share characteristics with real-world securities, such as rights conferred on the holder or expectation of a return, and are regulated. The actual use of the funds raised has no bearing on the designation of the token: rollercoaster tickets are utilities, regardless of whether or not the cash raised from their sale pays for construction work.

This flexibility and the reliance by regulators on principles and characteristics rather than strict rules give the UK a uniquely balanced set of guidelines for the emerging blockchain and cryptocurrency landscape, according to Martin Bartlam, International Group Head of Finance and Projects and FinTech Global Group Chair at DLA Piper. He is bemused by the enthusiasm of some startups to hop jurisdictions, setting up their business in Gibraltar, Switzerland, Malta, or Singapore to access different frameworks that they see as more suited to their needs despite their customer base being elsewhere. It is a sad indictment of the Magic Internet Money mindset that the priority is sometimes not solving a problem for the customer but avoiding problems for the entrepreneur. For most, though, the UK's approach to regulation is supportive of genuine innovation and viable business models and has its feet firmly in the real world.

Bartlam also observed that the volume of ICOs coming through the firm dropped off markedly even before the crypto bubble hit its peak at the end of 2017. As a result of market volatility, there is a trend now for the more viable businesses seeking ICO funds to offer stablecoin tokens for sale, which are tethered to real-world reserves of fiat currency or gold. This is a complicated process but is perceived as a better course of action than exposure to fluctuations in crypto valuations.

The Bank of England has also made changes that will have positive implications for cryptocurrency. Governor Mark Carney announced in June 2019 that nonbanks can hold an account with them, which initially impacts payment companies such as Worldpay, and was cautiously welcoming of the "systematically important" Libra whitepaper, which had been published a few days earlier. Launching accounts for nonbanks opens the door for stablecoins to store supporting reserves with the Bank of England, a positive signal for the integration of cryptocurrencies with mainstream finance. Carney has indicated more than once that he is supportive of cryptocurrencies in general. Speaking at a meeting of central bankers in Wyoming in August 2019,[13] he suggested that a global digital currency could become the world's reserve, releasing U.S. dollar funds from the role and insulating world economies from volatility in the United States.

France

Speaking at the Blockchain Game Summit in Lyon, France, in September 2019, lawyer Jean-Baptiste Soufron, former senior advisor on digital economy to the French Minister of Innovation, outlined the French approach to ICOs. A token sale to fund the development of a new platform, he explained, can be compared to buying a calf for a farmer's herd. The animal is essential to the business model and is viewed as a utility from the outset. It may take time to mature sufficiently to produce milk, and it may accrue value, but neither of these features should disqualify its consideration as a utility rather than a security.

This is the most flexible interpretation we have seen and comes from a jurisdiction which is largely supportive of ICOs. France has taken time to consult with the industry and define the practicalities around token sales. The PACTE law,[14] an action plan for the growth and transformation of business (plan d'action pour la croissance et la transformation des entreprises) was enacted in April 2019 and includes specific regulation surrounding ICOs (Offres de jetons virtuels). It recognizes that ICOs have become a key fundraising vehicle for innovative projects, and that it is important to distinguish the genuine offers from the fraudulent. Its guidelines include the use of a traditional escrow mechanism for the token sale process, proof of robust internal systems and insurances for the company, and a requirement for clear and accurate white papers, all intended to mitigate risk to investors.

Malta, Gibraltar, Singapore, and Zug

Several smaller states accelerated past more complex jurisdictions in the early days of this industry to establish themselves as champions of blockchain and cryptocurrency. They attracted attention from fundraisers seeking legislative endorsement and credibility for their ICOs in the gold rush years 2015 to 2017 and proposed early examples of specific regulations, which are gradually being passed into local law.

In its quest to become the capital of blockchain and cryptocurrency in Europe, Malta, the self-styled Blockchain Island, passed three bills in November 2018 around technology, tokens, and cryptocurrency. According to *Forbes* writer Rachel Wolfson, the Malta model takes a technology first approach and has developed a clear regulatory framework, recognizing the importance of legal certainty for businesses in the sector. The bills include certification for exchanges, which was a major factor in the relocation of leading exchange Binance to the island, a regulatory regime for ICOs, and a requirement for internal governance in distributed ledger technology to promote credibility.

From Crypto Island to Crypto Valley, the Swiss canton of Zug was an early haven for blockchain businesses and a welcoming jurisdiction for ICO fundraising when other countries were still developing their guidelines. More than 50 blockchain companies are now established in the region.

Gibraltar also pitched for the "blockchain island" crown, developing the first regulatory framework for distributed ledger technology, and establishing a series of nine principles to which DLT businesses on the peninsula are expected to subscribe.

Singapore's Securities and Futures Act governs utility and security tokens, while its Payment Services Act regulates what the British FCA would describe as Exchange Tokens.

Gibraltar, Malta, and Singapore historically inherited the British legal framework, for a variety of reasons, and the flexibility of their regulations has much in common with the balance that seems to have been achieved by the UK's FCA. After a torrid few years, the Gold Rush seems to be fading, and we are moving toward a more stable ecosystem with sustainable business models.

A Coin for Every Occasion

The United Nations recognizes 180 currencies as legal tender in the real world. By contrast, Cryptoslate[15] lists over 2,100 cryptocurrencies. The proliferation of coins in the digital world comes down to their nature: cryptocurrencies are programmable money. They can and do have specialist functions according to their place in the digital ecosystem. Many coins grease the wheels of their own distributed ledger, while others are tokens within Ethereum.

Tokens are a particularly interesting aspect of distributed ledger technology. A token is not just digital cash: it is programmable money. Tokens with different properties are commonly referred to by the reference number of the relevant Ethereum Request for Comment (ERC), which led to their development by the open-source community. The most common are ERC20 tokens, which act as native currency for applications built on the Ethereum blockchain. Other tokens have specialized roles: ERC721 and ERC1155 have been widely adopted to perform specific functions in gaming and are spilling over into the world of business, as we will see in Chapter 5. A token can be a measurement of value, a nonmonetary unique or generic asset, or a degree of influence in a community.

Let's have a look at some of the types of cryptocurrencies in circulation and their individual functions.

Anonymity and Privacy

Bitcoin, Ether, and other cryptocurrencies appear to the casual eye to be anonymous, with a user's wallet address rendered as a string of letters and numbers. This is not the case. They are not anonymous, but pseudonymous. It is entirely possible to trace transactions out to the real world. There are other coins, however, whose structure enables anonymity and privacy for users. The most prominent of these are Monero, Dash, and Zcash.

While any transaction on the Bitcoin blockchain identifies the sender, receiver, and amount for all to see, transactions involving privacy coins are obfuscated in a variety of ways. Mechanisms include hiding details of the transacting wallets, splitting payments into several separate amounts, disguising a genuine transaction in a list of decoys, and permissioned views. In effect, these coins replicate our day-to-day cash transactions: no transparent, public record can be interrogated to prove who passed a dollar bill to their friend.

Stablecoins

One of the greatest challenges for cryptocurrency is the volatility of Bitcoin, Ether, and their peers. Quite apart from bubbles such as 2017's tenfold rise in value and 2018's corresponding fall, the day-to-day fluctuations in cryptocurrency compared to large fiat currencies cause friction and challenges with adoption. While the crypto ecosystem is still small, there are too few transactions for value exchange (in other words, purchase of goods and services) compared to the volume of speculative trades, which drive dips and spikes in price. Even where there are flourishing areas of cryptocurrency use or popular applications, the exchange risk involved in moving back and forth to fiat is high. This friction at the edge is a substantial barrier to entry and tars perfectly sound distributed ledger applications with the brush of unpredictability.

Enter the stablecoin. This is a specific class of cryptocurrency whose value is not driven by the vagaries of the emerging cryptocurrency market but by the movements of real-world assets. There are several advantages to stablecoins, reducing friction at the edge of the crypto ecosystem by acting as a form of value airlock. For investors in cryptocurrency they represent a lifebelt within the crypto world, a safe haven in the event of extreme volatility. For existing users of public blockchain applications, they are becoming a link to the real world: in California, for example, it is now possible to pay state taxes from cannabis-related businesses in stablecoin. Finally, applications which use a stablecoin as their core cryptocurrency remove a large part of the perceived risk for new adopters, enabling people to benefit from blockchain-enabled applications without worries over volatility and liquidity.

The earliest and most widely adopted of a clutch of stablecoins, Tether is aligned to the value of the U.S. dollar and collateralized by its matching fiat currency reserves. Tether has suffered from bad press in the past, notably due to a lack of independent verification of its reserves. It also gained notoriety thanks to third party manipulative trading of Bitcoin to and from Tether, which may have artificially inflated the value of Bitcoin during the bull run of 2017.

The issue of trust and confidence is one which Cameron and Tyler Winklevoss of the Gemini exchange are addressing head on. The Gemini Dollar is the world's first regulated, audited stablecoin. The Winklevoss twins have a clear agenda of building trust through oversight, avoiding the very human problems that have plagued custodians in the cryptocurrency world. Speaking at the SXSW conference in Austin, Texas, in March 2019 they explained that "the most healthy markets are the best regulated" and reiterated that the key to success is "not the tech, it's the trust."

While Tether, Gemini, and other collateralized stablecoins have the onerous requirement to maintain matching reserves, DAI from MakerDAO (Maker) has overcome the need to hold physical reserves through automatic pricing systems built into the token's smart contracts.

These mechanisms are continually readjusting the price of DAI as the market fluctuates, ensuring that it remains pegged one-to-one with the U.S. dollar. Since its launch in 2017, it has demonstrated good stability despite major volatility in the market.

It is becoming more and more common for applications to be developed using a stablecoin as their principle currency, says Martin Bartlam of DLA Piper. Established apps are also turning to stablecoin. Tom Kysar of the Augur Project, which was one of the earliest Ethereum applications to be developed, explained that a need for lower volatility led version 2.0 of their peer-to-peer prediction market to move to trading in DAI. The mitigation of cryptocurrency risk has become a vital step toward greater blockchain adoption. However, there is a caveat: for all that this approach reassures new users whose concept of money is informed by fiat behavior, stablecoins are in danger of abandoning the systematic stability of traditional cryptocurrency in a quest for price stability.

Specialized Cryptocurrencies

In the world of financial technology (FinTech), the concept of a distributed ledger was quick to be explored. After all, financial systems are built on the checks and balances of ledgers and the industry both understood the new technology and realized that it may one day supplant traditional banking. Considerable work has been done in all areas of FinTech and banking to explore automation, decentralization, and the role of blockchain in managing trust between mutually suspicious parties.

So where are the FinTech coins? The largest of these is XRP, the native currency of the Ripple cross-border payment platform. Ripple has been adopted by banks worldwide and is a popular blockchain application aiming to reduce friction in international transfers. The fact that XRP is fundamental to the niche Ripple application has led to controversy and argument that XRP is not a decentralized cryptocurrency and should not be traded as such. Legal action around whether the sale of XRP on the open market was legitimate in the first place has been rumbling in the background. Despite this, XRP grew to be one of the more popular traded cryptos thanks to the widening adoption of Ripple. A spinoff from an XRP form, XLM is also gaining traction in the payment processing space.

Another coin with a niche application is IOTA, the native cryptocurrency of the eponymous blockchain, which focuses on the security of the Internet of Things and enabling machine-to-machine communication. IOTA's framework departs from Satoshi's blockchain structure, introducing a concept called Tangle. Transactions are written to the ledger and attached to others by an edge, rather than a linear chain. A transaction can only be entered if the node doing so validates two adjoining transactions. This results in a random consensus where, as more transactions are entered, more validations are completed, so in theory the system runs faster the more data is recorded. The validations use the same Hashcash basis as the Bitcoin blockchain but with a much lower level of complexity, which means that nodes can validate with limited processing power on smartphones or within sensors. The IOTA coin (more accurately mIOTA) is the means of payment for any machine-to-machine transactions which happen within the network. IOTA has still to be proven at scale, but it occupies an increasingly important niche in the world of blockchain and cryptocurrency.

Crypto for the Masses

Adoption of cryptocurrency has, unsurprisingly, been a worldwide phenomenon. According to the 2019 Statista Global Consumer Survey,[16] Turkish citizens led the way with 20 percent of those surveyed having owned or used cryptocurrency; Brazil, Columbia, Argentina, and South Africa also reported usage rates above 16 percent. This contrasts with much lower levels of adoption in Western Europe and North America (6 percent in the United Kingdom, 5 percent in the United States). Cryptocurrency is gaining ground as a genuine alternative medium for exchange of value in countries where there is volatility, heavily controlled currencies, or a large proportion of the population without access to banking facilities. This is not to say that adoption in such economies has been easy. Authorities have attempted to regulate and even ban cryptocurrency mining and use in a number of countries with varying degrees of success. In cultures where there is strong government control and censorship, exchanges which are permitted may be heavily regulated. Venezuela has been held up by some cryptocurrency evangelists as a pioneer thanks to the creation of a national cryptocurrency, the Petro, but the real picture is far more complex and sinister. There is a clear distinction between what Andreas M. Antonopoulos describes as "money of the people," that is open, borderless, neutral, censorship-resistant cryptocurrency, and "money of the government" under centralized control. Because no-one trusts the Petro, use of Bitcoin has flourished defiantly.

Cryptocurrency is gaining traction where it has utility for users: this is only to be expected. However, any enterprise introducing an application that incorporates the use of cryptocurrency must consider the mechanism by which they expand their user base beyond the crypto space.

Adoption Through Need

Case Study: Venezuela

My colleague Patricia O'Callaghan left Venezuela in 2017 in the face of mounting inflation, crumbling infrastructure, and dismal prospects for the future. The inflation rate at the time was reported by the International Monetary Fund to have reached 1,000,000 percent, with predictions that this would rise to an estimated 10 million percent in the following 12 months. Patricia and her friends, now scattered across the world, told me about the challenges of the environment they left behind and the importance of Bitcoin in Venezuelan society.

Cryptocurrency is viewed in countries with a stable banking and political system as a volatile, risky venture. In Venezuela, where people are facing rapid devaluation of the local currency, Bitcoin plays the role of a stablecoin. Individuals receiving payments in the local currency, the Bolivar, cannot convert to fiat currencies. Holding dollars is illegal, to the extent that Patricia recalls being stopped by the police and having the few dollars in her wallet confiscated. Conversion to Bitcoin became a way to preserve value, transfer money between citizens and across borders, and store savings safely: "Bitcoin is much safer than dollars," she explains.

Using Bitcoin is not as simple as we might expect given the reported uptake. A lack of reliable infrastructure results in regular power cuts, or more accurately a sporadic supply of electricity to one town, then another. Internet access is patchy or nonexistent. Bitcoin mining, once lucrative thanks to virtually free electricity funded by the country's oil revenues, is illegal. Any equipment found is confiscated, although this simply moves the mining rigs into the control of the government. But still Bitcoin flourishes. Payment for regular commodities in Bitcoin via SMS started to become common in November 2018, in grocery stores, restaurants, coffee shops, and even for buying clothes. This is a huge cultural shift in a country where very few people were previously aware of cryptocurrency and only a small population had access to the internet. The response to the political and economic situation has been a wholesale adoption of "money of the people."

What of the "money of the government"? The Petro is increasingly being imposed on a population who are not technologically able to cope with it. Pensions are paid in Petro, and a video, which circulated widely online, shows a tax collector demanding payment in Petro from a business owner.[17] The young man was unable to oblige, explaining that all his customers paid him in Bolivars, and was jailed for his protest. Many of the Venezuelan professional classes have left the country, including my developer colleague and her husband, a doctor. For those who leave, at least they can transfer their money out of the country in Bitcoin. On the Columbian border, easily reached on foot, there are Bitcoin ATMs in place ready for new arrivals to access their savings. Independent reports also suggest that the main users of Columbia's growing Athena Bitcoin ATM network are Venezuelans transferring cash back home.[18]

The most effective adoption of any new technology is that driven by need, and true cryptocurrencies, emerging as they have from the Crypto Anarchist ethos, are perfectly suited to meet a need such as that of Venezuelan citizens and others around the world in a similar position. What, then, are the incentives in a society without an obvious need for a "money of the people"?

Putting the User First

A Seamless User Experience

It is much easier to bring users on board through the familiar. People may not realize that they are using cryptocurrency at all thanks to centralized structures that have custodianship of assets. Blockchain and cryptocurrency innovator Adryenn Ashley outlines the pattern of technology adoption through recent history. The VHS versus Betamax video formats was a battle won by the less robust but more familiar VHS: after all, reasoned consumers, this was just a big cassette tape. CDs became mainstream for audio, smoothing the path for DVDs as a new medium for video despite the technical superiority of laser discs. Cryptocurrency adoption relies upon this appeal to familiarity, says Ashley. If the language is too alien, or the methods of access too complex, then there is no path for the mainstream consumer to follow.

Adoption Through Play

Gaming is one area where cryptocurrency can add new functionality without disrupting the user experience. As many as 250 million Fortnite players pay to play using VBucks in the game, and World of Warcraft's WoW Gold and off-platform asset trading is well established. Onboarding new cryptocurrency users through play gives users the chance to own their coins and assets, but why should the user's experience be disrupted? Gaming industry veteran Alex Amsel discussed this challenge with me. He also sees the challenge of introducing the benefits of cryptocurrency without compromising the existing features to which the gaming community are accustomed. Stablecoins provide a route to eliminating volatility, but there is no reason why games should not be denominated in fiat currency, and this is increasingly the route being taken.

Adoption by Informed Choice

Crypto-Maximalism

Crypto-maximalists advocate for a future where people consciously opt to have absolute decentralized control of their own assets, following in the footsteps of the Cypherpunks and the crypto-anarchist vision. These may include users who are otherwise unbanked or do not wish to place their trust in government, but to actively adopt cryptocurrency implies a degree of knowledge and understanding of the crypto landscape and language. To expand this way requires user education and a considerable amount of work to improve the public perception of cryptocurrency. In those cases where cryptocurrency has been directly adopted, for example among groups of Venezuelan citizens, this is driven by need but still requires understanding.

Education is an important part of giving users the choice to use cryptocurrency. Understanding the pros and cons of controlling crypto assets improves safe and secure use and helps to promote appropriate adoption where cryptocurrency meets a need.

Educating Asia

Direct interaction with a potential user base and proactive education and onboarding are gradually driving adoption in Asia in the face of regulation, censorship, and anti-crypto propaganda. Emily Rose Dallara, Head of Marketing and Growth of trading platform Liquid.com, has worked throughout Asia and is based in Saigon, Vietnam. She observes that Tokyo, along with Bangkok, is probably the most advanced in adoption, where Roger Ver, Akane Yokoo, and their team have encouraged a large volume of small businesses to take Bitcoin Cash (BCH) both in person and online. It's now possible to make micropurchases in coffee shops and restaurants across the Tokyo central districts of Roppongi and Shibuya, and it is becoming increasingly straightforward for an online merchant to accept BCH.

The adoption that Dallara sees among Vietnamese traders is more likely to be driven by holders of cryptocurrency encouraging others to use it so they can spend their money. Accepting crypto can also present problems for merchants as it is illegal to ask for payment or list prices in any currency other than the Vietnamese Dong (VND), and across Asia there are so many e-money applications in use that crypto is just another payment option. However, there is one area where cryptocurrencies are meeting a need, albeit one that will not find favor with the authorities. Vietnam, in common with many other more centralized, communist countries, discourages the transfer of VND out of the country. Dallara's experience is that it is easier and cheaper to convert VND to BCH on a local exchange and manage cross-border transfers in cryptocurrency.

In Saigon there is also a big focus on the DAI stablecoin, and people have started accepting cryptocurrencies online and converting to DAI or USD. How this gradual adoption plays out against the political backdrop of Asia's communist countries will be interesting.

One cultural aspect that sometimes escapes Western eyes is that being unbanked in Asia is neither unusual nor a disadvantage. Our economy expects people to have access to traditional banking and excludes those who do not, for instance, by offering more competitive utility pricing to those who can pay by direct debit from their bank. The advantage we might expect to accrue to the unbanked in Western culture is not going to drive adoption in the East.

Banking the Unbanked

Gaining access to a store of value and payment mechanism is attractive for those who are disadvantaged by being unbanked, and for cash economies such as the emerging cannabis industry. Cryptocurrency fills a vacuum where banks cannot or will not step in, whether this is a result of external regulation or their internal business model. This is a problem close to home. According to Federal Deposit Insurance Corporation research,[19] 6.5 percent of U.S. households are unbanked, and a further 18.7 percent underbanked, representing 32.6 million households in the largest economy on the planet. If these households were able to use cryptocurrencies as easily as bank customers use fiat currencies, this would reduce economic exclusion.

Case Study: Abstrakt

Companies such as Austin-based Abstrakt are already working toward this goal, aiming to make cryptocurrency use uncomplicated and secure. Speaking to founder Corey Segall, he reinforces the need for a straightforward user experience to help adoption while ensuring that the individual has ownership of their assets and data. Banking clients and users of payment mechanisms such as PayPal have access to good mobile applications, which enable quick and easy transactions: why should this be any different with cryptocurrency? The challenge, of course, is that where a user holds the keys to the safe, they have full responsibility for the security of the assets. If mistakes are made in banking, or on any platform where there is good custodianship, there is recourse to a centralized ledger. If individual users make mistakes in the management of crypto assets, for instance sending funds to the wrong wallet, or worse, losing the private keys which are the sole means of access to your assets, then there is no way back.

Abstrakt's proprietary technology is available publicly as the VaultWallet mobile app but is more usually found under the hood of a number of fintech and blockchain applications. It addresses these two worst case scenarios of cryptocurrency use with outwardly simple transactions (from whom, to whom, and how much) backed up by innovative sharded key management strategies and automatic server-side fraud detection mechanisms. The focus is on delivering a high level of security for the user from several angles. The system is protected against direct attacks by its distributed nature, against fraud through confirmatory signing if the transaction is clean, and against user error with a series of backup options, which are carefully designed to avoid any custodian relationship arising. Ultimately, says Segall, for day-to-day transactions users should experience the same ease of use with cryptocurrency as they have with their credit card or checking account.

Libra: A New Pathway?

In June 2019, the publication of the Libra white paper by Facebook opened a new channel for cryptocurrency adoption, and according to Andreas M. Antonopoulos,[20] brought into being a third construct: "money of the corporation." It had long been speculated that at least one of the Silicon Valley giants would bring out its own cryptocurrency, with work going on not only at Facebook but at Amazon, Apple, and Google; this whitepaper was the first shot across the bows of traditional banking. The launch of Libra was originally planned for mid-2020, subject to production and regulatory hiccups, but the project suffered early setbacks with the withdrawal of major founding members including Paypal, Visa, Mastercard and Stripe. Despite this, the publication of the Libra whitepaper was significant for several reasons.. First, it changed the dynamic between cryptocurrency and banking overnight, making a worldwide user base of two billion and a wider public aware of an alternative to "money of the government" backed by a recognized brand. It represented more of a threat to banks than to established decentralized currencies, which regulators were not slow to recognize. Second, it was designed to be a seamlessly accessible medium for peer-to-peer payment. Once ease of use of a corporate currency is established across a large population, the world of traditional cryptocurrencies opens up to users who are more discerning about privacy, neutrality, and value conferred by the community rather than by a basket of fiat currencies.

Widespread cryptocurrency adoption will be influenced by corporate cryptocurrencies, but there are many more factors at play, along with considerations for the protection of individual users and the practicality of using digital cash in the real world. Let's look more closely at the custodians of cryptocurrency and ways of reducing friction at the edges of the crypto ecosystem.

The Contradiction of Custodianship

From cryptocurrency's anarchic beginnings, the intention was that Bitcoin and those coins that followed should be money of the people, decentralized and unfettered by agency or authority. The people had other ideas. As the equipment required to mine cryptocurrencies became prohibitively expensive and enthusiasts sought to invest in this new asset, exchanges sprang up to meet the need of buyers and sellers whose early transactions were clandestine face-to-face meetings for cash purchase of digital goods. Of course, once coins could be purchased through a digital intermediary the temptation for new investors was to leave their coins on the exchange. This was the curse of the familiar: exchanges began to be treated as de facto banks. It is ironic that while the Bitcoin white paper was published in the wake of the 2007 to 2008 banking crash and offered a decentralized alternative, the increasing numbers of Bitcoin holders turned toward what looked like traditional structures to manage their accounts.

Risks of Individual Control

Cryptocurrency holders are encouraged by the community to move their assets from exchange wallets to private storage, and on January 3, 2019 the first "Proof of Keys" event took place. This date, the tenth anniversary of the Bitcoin Genesis Block, was chosen as a reminder for holders to be sure they had private keys for all of their assets and to move long-term investment coins into more secure private storage. For newer entrants, this felt like jumping out of the frying pan and into the fire, a step out of the familiarity of bank-like exchanges to a new world of holding your money in what amounts to a digital personal safe. But even if you have control of all your assets, are they really as secure as they can possibly be?

Even the most careful cryptocurrency investors have fallen foul of manipulation and theft from their private wallets, to say nothing of the Bitcoins which have been lost down the back of the virtual sofa over the years thanks to misplaced keys, destruction of records, or accidentally junked hardware. Cryptocurrency theft is a growing phenomenon, particularly where hackers exploit the security around individually held assets to gain entry. In November 2018 a group of investors sued both AT&T and T-Mobile for negligence in allowing the SIM cards on their accounts to be replaced in response to verbal requests from hackers.[21] The replacement SIM cards were then used to pass two-factor authentication controls and access wallets: one victim reportedly lost 3 million unspecified coins, while another quantified the loss at the time at $621,000.

Investors are caught between the risk of trusting a centralized exchange with their decentralized assets, and the risk of disaster in their own hands for which there is little or no recourse. Cryptocurrency cannot scale effectively with this degree of risk associated. How can we move forward?

Watching the Watchmen

Exchanges may have been free of centralized government regulation, but they have been historically equally free of any exacting or enforceable standards to protect the consumer. For many people the risks involved in remaining on an exchange are outweighed by fear of the complexity and precision required to move funds to wallets under their sole control. Exchanges have been trusted to watch over significant holdings of cryptocurrency on behalf of individuals, resurrecting an age-old question. A little short of two thousand years ago, Roman poet Juvenal coined the phrase "Quis custodiet ipsos custodes?": Who watches the watchmen? This is a legitimate concern. In February 2014 the highest volume exchange of the time, Mt Gox, suffered a record theft which ultimately brought down the organization as thousands of holdings were compromised and a staggering 850,000 Bitcoin were stolen, although some were later recovered. Despite efforts by exchanges to build trust and establish self-regulation, a second scandal emerged almost five years later. Canadian company Quadriga Fintech Solutions originally hit the headlines in 2015 as potentially the world's first publicly traded Bitcoin exchange.[22] The plans to list were shelved soon after this announcement, but coming as it did in the wake of Mt Gox, the publicity helped Quadriga's reputation as a business that expressed a wish to be regulated. In January 2019 following some financial challenges, it was reported that founder Gerald Cotten had died suddenly without leaving instructions for access to the cold (offline) wallets holding all the funds deposited on the exchange. Suspicions raised at the time about the circumstance of the loss and the certification of Cotten's passing in India were vindicated when auditors discovered that the wallets had been emptied some weeks prior to the founder's disappearance. During the long court investigation which followed, Ernst and Young observed that the "operating structure was significantly flawed from a financial reporting and operational control perspective."[23] If self-regulation falls at the first hurdle, what trust can be placed in custodians?

Case Study: Gemini

Cameron and Tyler Winklevoss, founders of the Gemini exchange, sit firmly in the camp of externally regulated custodianship. As seasoned crypto investors they watched the development of the space including the high-profile exchange disasters and increasingly frequent reports of theft from both exchanges and individuals. This prompted them to act. In most of these cases, they observed at their SXSW 2019 keynote, the weak link has been human: the trust placed in the guardians of crypto assets has been misplaced.

Who watches the watchmen? they asked the audience. In the absence of caped heroes, the Winklevoss twins assert that regulatory oversight is currently our only hope. They argue that the healthiest financial markets are those with the best regulation, and that regardless of the currency involved, the future of money requires trust. They started work on their Gemini exchange in the aftermath of the Mt Gox collapse and acquired their banking license before launching. Gemini's founders have their eyes on long term security for investors and long-term success for the business, once again comparing the development of the cryptocurrency space with the historic rise of the internet. They reminded the audience about early legal wrangles between Microsoft and Netscape, which held those 1990s giants back from dominance on the internet, allowing Google to overtake. The Winklevoss twins are in the exchange business for the long haul, ready to take the opportunity that being a trusted custodian should convey.

Defining Stability

Critics have said in the past that "you can't buy your coffee with Bitcoin." As we have seen, this is no longer the case in Tokyo, Caracas, Bangkok, and hundreds of cities around the world, but the trope illustrates a fundamental challenge for cryptocurrency: its volatility when compared to fiat currency. We are generally used to a $3 coffee today being a $3 coffee tomorrow. We take home our regular pay, and budget for the month accordingly. Surely it's unreasonable to adopt a system where coffee is $3 today, $6 tomorrow, and $1 the day after? In some places, this is the norm. Friends who lived in Zimbabwe during its prolonged periods of economic instability recall walking into the store and not knowing whether the bread would be 20 cents or $5 that day. Patricia O'Callaghan's father still works in banking in Venezuela: I have seen video of thousands of notes being fed into the bank shredder, replaced by a new issue after only two years as legal tender. Government money is not systematically stable and relies upon the mechanism of fiscal policy to bestow price stability.

Cryptocurrency is the opposite of government money. As Wall Street veteran Caitlin Long explained following a flurry of price movements in June 2019,[24] Bitcoin was designed for systematic stability, not for price stability, and the two concepts are probably mutually exclusive. Demand for money itself is not stable, influenced by factors from natural disasters to population growth through regulation, industrial developments, and seasonal changes. Basic economic theory of demand and supply suggests that in periods of high demand the price of a scarce commodity should rise, but, as Long says, "central bankers manufacture the price stability of fiat currencies by interfering with natural market processes."

Systematic stability is quite different. As demand for Bitcoin rises, there is no way to increase the supply of coins to match demand and maintain price, because the number of Bitcoin is fixed. Instead, the security of the system varies with demand through an automatic increase in the difficulty of the mining algorithm. How can government money, manipulated for price stability and suppression of market volatility, maintain systematic stability? As Long observes, interference can only result in instability. Since the 1980s, she observes, "traditional financial markets have ping-ponged within a crisis/stability/crisis cycle." Day-to-day, we might enjoy the price stability that government money gives us, but cryptocurrency offers an alternative systematically stable route, which will have its day in times of crisis.

In the search for mechanisms to improve the uptake of cryptocurrency people can lose sight of the fundamental role of money as an honest ledger, a way of recording transactions in a way that the community accepts. Bitcoin has claimed its place as a monetary unit precisely because the community accorded it a value and used it to record the buying and selling of real-world assets. In Venezuela, the price of Bitcoin against the dollar is irrelevant. Venezuelans have had enough volatility in their government-issued fiat currency, and the fact that Bitcoin is gaining traction in day-to-day purchasing shows it is valued as a means of exchange.

Ultimately, there is no quick fix. For traders and consumers to embrace cryptocurrency, there must be a real advantage over the status quo. This could be triggered by price instability in traditional fiat currencies, by a community's decision to use a cryptocurrency as its honest ledger of transaction value, or by the increased adoption of blockchain outside the monetary system. With that in mind, let's turn to the ways in which the technology underpinning cryptocurrency is solving problems in the wider world.

CHAPTER 4

That's Not My Tuna

The clink of glasses cuts through the cacophony of friends and new acquaintances chattering around the room. Waiters move smoothly through the crowd offering trays of sushi to the assembled guests. Looking at the selection of rice parcels on offer, a woman picks up her phone and scans a barcode on the tray. Within seconds, the app shows her where the tuna on this sushi has been fished, and confirms its sustainable, regulated source. She smiles, picks up a piece and pops in in her mouth. "Delicious."

Fact or fiction? At the ConsenSys Ethereal conference in New York in November 2018, the provenance of the tuna on the sushi served for guests was authenticated through an Ethereum application. The tuna scenario is a commonly cited exemplar of how a distributed supply chain ledger can deliver value over and above that already achieved with traditional technology. In the fully realized future, transparent records which can be independently authenticated via an immutable, independent source will give regulators confidence. Prime entry from sensors in the widening Internet of Things will mitigate human error and reduce the risk of deliberate falsification of records, ensuring that raw materials originate from a regulated source and that goods are transported under the right conditions. Hashed identity and qualification records will allow secure and reliable verification of current permits for people at every stage. It is a compelling vision of the future value of blockchain, and the building blocks are already in place in the present.

Business Adoption of Distributed Ledgers

The journey toward realization of a digital currency did not happen in a vacuum. The evolution of software tools, process automation and the World Wide Web, and the strides both in developing strong cryptography and bringing it out of government control, have had enormous relevance to business. Peer-to-peer networks developed before cryptocurrencies, and enterprise has always had to deal with mutually suspicious groups and maintaining the security of commercially sensitive and personally confidential information, but blockchain adds a new dimension. The publication of the Bitcoin white paper inspired not only cryptocurrency enthusiasts but also innovators who identified the underlying structure as a solution to some of their business problems.

Professor Mike Smith was one such innovator. During our wide-ranging discussion, Smith told me that after reading the Satoshi whitepaper in 2011 he found that the concept resonated with him. He dabbled briefly in mining and narrowly avoided the 2014 collapse of the Mt Gox cryptocurrency exchange, but a business challenge crystallized for him the real value of blockchain. A Scandinavian data protectorate approached one of his clients with an informal complaint that data the business collected for mental health assessments was being altered after collection. This was not the case, although data smoothing is common practice in multiple industries. Smoothing is used to expose trends and key indicators in data sets that may be noisy or peppered with extremes. Smith's focus, however, has always been on retaining raw data in its original form, both for its base integrity and the future usefulness of the information.

The challenge was to prove to the complainants that the data was stored exactly as collected. Smith had already tested the principle that 256-bit hashing produces a unique string from any data, and therefore started out by concatenating all the timestamped data sets collected in a single day and generating a hash. The hash of the second day's data was then recursively hashed with the previous day's string to give each day positional integrity in a chain: a timestamped blockchain. Finally, the hashes were broadcast on three different websites, because "multiple transmissions of data keep people honest." The regulators were able to verify that the data was unchanged, and the complaint was quietly shelved.

This simple application is reflected in the most successful uses of blockchain: it is a great example of a problem being solved in the most appropriate way. The greatest threat to the reputation of distributed ledger technology is enterprise defaulting to blockchain as a silver bullet, manipulating the solution to fit, and losing sight of the original problem in the process.

Do You Really Need a Blockchain?

The cry that is guaranteed to strike despair into the heart of a responsible software developer is "we need a blockchain." When an organization sees a problem cantering toward it from the horizon, a knee-jerk reaction is often to look to the newest technologies for a solution. A classic example of this is the reaction of the Philip Hammond, then Chancellor of the Exchequer in the British government, during the protracted negotiations around the United Kingdom's proposed exit from the European Union (Brexit) in October 2018. Faced with the almost insurmountable challenge of securing a frictionless land border between the UK and European Union on the island of Ireland, he clutched at the straws of emerging technology as a way to maintain the existing freedom of movement and avoid imposing border controls in a historically difficult location.[1] "There is technology becoming available," he said. "I don't claim to be an expert on it, but the most obvious technology is blockchain." He is not alone in making the erroneous assumption that a new problem has to be solved by new technology. The reputation of blockchain as a valid option in a broad toolkit of potential solutions has suffered from fundamental misunderstandings as to its nature and its limitations.

City Web Consultants is a software development company with experience in deploying a range of traditional and emerging technologies to meet client requirements. Its founder Adam Clarey has over the years watched a string of new concepts and ideas move from a state of overhyped excitement to disillusionment when the promise is not realized. Occasionally the business is approached by people who just have their eyes on making magic internet money at little risk to themselves. Some proposals have no business model to speak of, driven by a desire simply to use the technology and present a "solution" where there is no problem to solve. Others have a genuine business proposition but have jumped at a buzzword rather than working through the logical process of identifying the most appropriate technology to deliver what they need. Blockchain is unlikely to be the solution: in most cases, the real challenge is to define the client's processes more clearly. Clarey is generally skeptical of the hype. "I have yet to come across any real-world project that truly benefits from using blockchain over any traditional technology," he says.

The excitement that overtook blockchain, as distinct from contemporary technologies, was largely due to the fundraising opportunities in the ICO gold rush. Clarey reflects on the madness of that period:

> During the boom of 2017 so much silly money was being pumped into blockchain / crypto projects that people's greed got the better of them. Those "investors" overlooked the basic business models and/ or underlying technology within these projects as [an ICO] was seen as a way to make large returns on their investment… I lost count of how many times I heard "blockchain will be the next internet." Silly rabbits. Since the bubble burst and people got burned, investors and businesses are now far more cautious and critical. Money is only flowing where there might be a genuine use-case for the technology.

The decline in easy ICO fundraising has brought good projects to the fore, where transparency and immutability can deliver real benefits and using a distributed ledger is an effective solution to the right problem. Blockchain is especially relevant where parties who do not know each other and have no intermediary need a mechanism to trust the recorded data. This need could arise because of a failure of systems of governance, or where consumers outside a supply chain want to confirm the source of a raw material, or where there is a need for trust between commercial organizations without any direct business relationship. It may also involve digital asset ownership, custodianship and exchange, reward mechanisms, and any automation that requires decentralization. Process efficiencies are being achieved using blockchain over traditional software, most notably in asset tracking, simple supply chains, and administrative tasks involving multiple parties. There are even some business models that have been proposed in the past but never realized and can now be achieved with the application of distributed ledger technology. There is a shift occurring from disillusionment to practical applications as blockchain claims its place in the technology landscape.

Blockchain Applications in the Real World

From processing, mining, harvesting, or manufacturing of products through to their consumption by the end consumer, blockchain applications are springing up in the most unexpected corners. While a seamless network of transparent ledgers spanning the globe is still the preserve of futurist fiction, there are commercial systems in place for authentication in the food supply chain, for provenance of luxury goods, and for elements of transportation, among others. Behind the scenes, administrative functions are being overhauled thanks to this technology, which enables transparency and collaboration between mutually suspicious groups. In particular, the financial services sector has been quick to identify those aspects of robotic process automation which would benefit from decentralization, and relationships with other industries such as the legal profession where trust is a factor in the smooth running of systems. Banking and auditing functions are working on a variety of blockchain applications, which range from small proofs of concept to deployed and scaling systems.

In the world of large capital projects, both public and private, blockchain models are improving the record keeping for complex supply chains and for decision approvals from design intent through construction and operation. The long-term nature of infrastructure projects, which may endure for decades, if not centuries, means that reliance on corporate knowledge and individual memory is unreliable, and assets may pass through several hands over their lifetime. Authentication of information is essential across the whole lifecycle of a capital asset.

Let's look in more detail at some of the new business practices that have been enabled by blockchain technology across all these sectors and examine the requirements for a successful blockchain implementation.

Getting to the Truth

One of the greatest misunderstandings of the nature of blockchain is that it is a repository of absolute truth. Yes, the immutability of the records held within the blockchain ensures that transactions are protected by what Joseph Lubin, part of the original Ethereum team and founder of ConsenSys, describes as "military-grade tamper resistance." You can be confident that a transaction or document authenticated by reference to a blockchain record is original and unchanged. But what is the subject of the transaction? In the case of cryptocurrency, coins are generated from within the construct and the transactions recorded relate to assets whose provenance is certain. As soon as you step outside the virtual world and start to represent the physical in digital form, how can you be sure that the asset making its immutable way through these decentralized ledgers is the right one?

Reliable Prime Entry: Garbage In, Garbage Out

You cannot trust everything that a computer tells you. For decades programmers have lived by the "GIGO" principle: if the inputs into any system are garbage, then what you get out, however good the processing in between, will also be garbage. Self-styled digital troublemaker Terence Eden applied the principle when attending an early talk by the team behind an art certification and verification platform. What if, he wondered, artwork being tracked by the blockchain was not the valuable original but a deliberately authenticated fake? His blog describes his spur-of-the-moment test of this concept during the company's presentation, accessing an early demonstration version of the platform.[2] "Long story short," he explains, "I convinced them that I painted the Mona Lisa. For this 'proof' I provided ... An e-mail address [and] a photo of the Mona Lisa from Wikipedia."

It is important to recognize that Verisart is working toward reliable physical and digital verification of provenance and that the platform is now being used commercially in the art and collectibles market, but Eden's prank highlighted clearly and simply that without trustworthy prime entry, blockchain records are not worth the data bits they occupy. The blockchain guarantees the truth of transactions, not absolute truth. For businesses that operate in the physical world there is a need to minimize or eliminate the risk of human error and deliberate interference at the point of data entry, making it more inconvenient to defraud the system than to maintain its integrity. Much of the work to be done will rely on behavioral change and incentives to be more rigorous in ensuring the accuracy of transactions, and this is already being observed in some blockchain implementations (for an example, see the Kraken IM case study later in this chapter). To tighten up our blockchain records, we can turn for help to other emerging technologies.

Intersection with the Internet of Things and Artificial Intelligence

The Internet of Things (IoT) introduces connectivity into everyday physical items, from smart kettles to intelligent buildings. Ondrej Vlcek, CTO and president of cybersecurity provider Avast, estimates that there will be up to 50 billion consumer devices online by 2025, to say nothing of the billions of commercial sensors, tools, vehicles, and machines that are rolling out rapidly as data connectivity improves, particularly with the introduction of 5G networks in major economies.

These sensors offer two things. First, the wealth of data that they collect gives deep insights into the behavior of the world and people within it. This informs and trains artificial intelligence (AI) to identify anomalies; AI is already being used in fraud detection, reducing the risk of inaccurate data making its way into centralized or decentralized ledgers. Second, direct communication from sensors to the ledger removes the human interface entirely. This is a key element of the IOTA blockchain discussed in previous chapters and is essential to the reliable operation of many enterprise blockchains.

Plenty of blockchain-integrated IoT scenarios have been suggested by researchers. One notable example from Huckle, Bhattacharya, White, and Beloff [3] follows a commuter journey, with a connected vehicle autonomously arranging its routing to refuel (or recharge), while the blockchain application confirms the identity of the driver, triggers the car to set up the preferred driving position for that individual, and enables payment for fuel using a smart contract without human intervention.

Case Study: National Archive

One particularly interesting combination of artificial intelligence and blockchain has been piloted by the UK's National Archives in association with the University of Surrey and the Open Data Institute. The work of the ARCHANGEL project on underscoring archival authenticity with blockchain,[4] published in 2019, has not only demonstrated a solution to an archiving challenge but may have greater impact on authentication of other media. Mark Bell of the National Archives told me more about this two-year project. The team started out experimenting with blockchain use cases in archiving. One of the challenges laid down by the Archives was how to manage the rapid change in media used for the recording and storage of video footage. Even as consumers, in our lifetimes we have seen camcorder tapes of family events converted to VHS, then DVD, then MP4. How can we be sure that the childhood footage we view on MP4 is the same as the tape made in the heady days of a 1970s summer?

The authentication of a record by comparing hashes is well established and already in use for born-digital records. Any such files are hashed on sending and verified on receipt as they move through departments, as part of a centralized process. One of the blockchain challenges addressed by the team looked at applying the same technique for independent, decentralized verification of original university research data years after publication. Video records present a far more complex problem. How do you verify content when you move from format to format, or from high to low resolution? The hash of a VHS video will be different to the hash of an identical, uncompromised MP4 even when the content is the same, because the formatting data causes a variation in the record. This is where artificial intelligence comes in to enhance the solution.

The ARCHANGEL team introduced content-aware deep learning to strip away the format-specific data within a record and isolate the footage beneath. Every version of the video record has a hash related to the original, and the common content is the traceable hash which runs through the archive. Blockchain comes into play when the transparency of records requires an immutable public chain of evidence. This is an excellent example of two complementary technologies playing to their strengths. There are also nuances to this implementation of blockchain which are specific to the National Archives. Some of the records they hold are embargoed for decades under British law: Census data, for instance, is released a full century after collection. In this context, even file names can be sensitive. This requires a permissioned structure, and ARCHANGEL is currently using Ethereum, with open and closed records and a Proof of Authority consensus.

The team also ran a trial with international archives, including the National Archives and Records Administration (NARA) in the United States, agencies in Estonia, Norway, Australia, and the National Records of Scotland. This substantial element of the work captured standard hashes of archived documents and demonstrated the necessarily collaborative nature of blockchain.

Bell points out that when work started on the project in 2016 the aim was simply to develop reliable authentication for the Archives' video records. Over the intervening years, the scandal of deep fake video has emerged, and the question of authenticity has been thrust into the public eye. This is an obvious next step for the research team,[5] whose solutions for verifying footage under their control can be turned to the task of identifying fraudulent content. It is refreshing to find an emerging problem which invites an emerging technology solution.

Provenance and Authenticity

We have already seen the work being done in authentication and verification of art and collectibles. Goods that are scarce and highly valued are a magnet for counterfeiting, and blockchain is helping to fight the fraudsters. Achieving reliable proof of authenticity is the problem, and accurate prime entry combined with immutable digital verification delivers a solution.

London's award-winning Everledger[6] pioneered the tracking of legally mined diamonds using forensics and digital asset twinning on a hybrid public/private distributed ledger framework. The physical attributes of a diamond are already recorded by laboratories, defining up to 40 different data points to produce a unique digital fingerprint. This is hashed to Everledger's Diamond Time-Lapse protocol, where more than a million individual, unique diamonds have already been recorded. Of course, representing a physical diamond digitally is something that could be replicated, but the complexity of the task is enormous. When the cost of being a bad actor is greater than the possible return, the system has inherent behavioral security. Of course, there is a strong commercial thread to this development. Everledger's work has huge implications for the insurance industry because accurate identification of diamonds is a weapon in the war against fraudulent claims. According to financial markets commentator Chris Skinner,[7] 65 percent of fraudulent diamond claims go undetected. Validating the provenance of a diamond delivers confidence in its origins, strikes a blow against illegal mining and its terrible social repercussions, and provides a digital proof of ownership.

Top fashion brands Louis Vuitton and Parfums Christian Dior, under their parent umbrella of LVMH, have collaborated with ConsenSys and Microsoft to develop the Aura platform, launched in May 2019.[8] Their goal is to give the consumer confidence and maintain the value of their premium brand. Aura "ensures the authenticity of the product, provides details on product origin and components (including ethical and environmental information), instructions for product care, and the after-sales and warranty services available." Aura was a natural extension of the Louis Vuitton Track and Trace program, building trustless authentication into the model. Not only has the company embraced blockchain, but it has opened up Aura to other luxury brands, recognizing the need for collaboration to fight the endemic fraud and counterfeiting in this sector.

Creation to Consumption

Tuna, Mangos and More

The supply chain is frequently cited as a perfect use-case for distributed ledger technology. Increased scrutiny of the origins of manufactured items, concerns for the environmental impact of the things that we use, and differing standards of health and safety, quality, or employment practices across the world, can be resolved by improved transparency and traceability. Potentially, every step of the way from raw material to finished product could be recorded and authenticated through blockchain. By tracking the provenance of components, ingredients, and materials, the purchaser can be confident that goods meet every relevant quality standard and that they are the genuine article. The potential to reduce counterfeiting and raise standards is significant. Combining a straightforward provenance chain with smart contracts smooths the cashflow of the participants, even across borders. This application of blockchain technology is possibly the furthest advanced, with multiple systems in active development and some at a stage of client readiness.

The tuna supply chain scenario envisages the involvement of multiple mutually suspicious parties from fishing to regulators to transport to processors to wholesale and finally to the consumer. The current state of supply chains involves trust relationships and regular verification of data. Businesses are always looking for a competitive edge, and this could be achieved in several ways. They might expand the supply chain beyond trusted parties, reduce the costs and the administrative burden of verification and regulation, or appeal to the consumer with greater transparency around sustainability, source, and authenticity. Blockchain is one tool that can facilitate these business model changes.

The first step in establishing a reliable digital record is to trace the physical asset and capture its movements in a way that can be relied upon. Supply chains already have the workflow in place to trace goods, and regulators rely upon the records kept and their own inspections to ensure that our clothes are not being made in factories that breach health and safety laws, or that tuna is being fished from the right waters by registered fleets. The difference that blockchain makes is locking the records into a distributed ledger and enabling them to be quickly authenticated by actors in the chain who do not have a direct relationship with either the organization or the individual who posted the data.

Distributed ledger supply chains are being developed and tested around the globe, and in October 2018 the IBM Food Trust[9] blockchain went live as a commercial product. During the proof of concept phase, IBM worked with Walmart who challenged them to trace two mangos from farm to store. Using existing systems this process took almost a week to run, while the blockchain-based system completed the task in 2.2 seconds.[10] Since then, IBM Food Trust systems have been adopted by other North American store chains, notably Albertson's,[11] and organizations including the National Fisheries Institute.[12] In Thailand, exporters of the legendary durian fruit are working with DiMuto, a Singapore-based startup, to transform fresh durians into traceable digital assets, tracking each individual fruit along the supply chain.[13]

It's early days in such a complex area and there are many issues to overcome, not least that, as we already know, a blockchain is only as good at the data that is fed into it. This is already being addressed by organizations in the sector, from the largest players to businesses like London-based startup AgriLedger, whose holistic approach to the value chain begins with Haitian farmers. When reliable inputs are overlaid with transparency and trust, this has implications for proof of ethical sourcing, distribution of wealth through the mechanism of smart contracts, and a reduction of opportunities for fraud and corruption.

Fighting Fake Pharmaceuticals

The provenance of commodities in the health supply chain is particularly sensitive as counterfeiting and human error in producing pharmaceuticals can have a direct impact on patient safety. The industry was quick to recognize the potential of blockchain to tackle the problem of compromised and fake medicines. According to Clauson et al. in a 2018 paper published in *Blockchain in Healthcare Today*,[14] not only the supply chain but the security of medical devices had the potential to be improved with blockchain applications, but at the time most initiatives were still in a proof of concept or pilot phase. This is still largely the case, but with increasingly substantial commercial and regulatory backing. Legislation has made drug traceability a strategic priority for pharmaceutical companies, including the 2013 enactment of the U.S. Drug Supply Chain Security Act (DSCSA). The 2023 deadline for compliance has pushed forward the development of new processes, and blockchain is at the heart of pilot projects with IBM, KPMG, Merck, and Walmart, according to Rachel Wolfson writing in *Forbes* in June 2019.[15] Walmart, whose Health and Wellness sales accounted for $35 billion of their U.S. revenues in 2018, is a staunch supporter of blockchain technology and has also stepped in to join the MediLedger consortium, another group focused on pharmaceutical tracking.

Why is blockchain a suitable solution to this problem? The fragmented nature of the U.S. medical industry, reported Wolfson, makes a decentralized system the most appropriate structure, ensuring transparency and trust for multiple parties from manufacturers to consumers. Blockchain satisfies the needs of mutually suspicious parties who want trusted information presented on a transparent (albeit permissioned) platform.

Crossing Oceans, Crossing Borders

Any implementation of new technology in an enterprise must confer a benefit, and the introduction of Insurwave, a blockchain-based system for shipping insurance, is a case in point. Freight giants A.P. Moller–Maersk faced a challenge in managing the complex ecosystem of the purchasing and administration of their highly transactional insurance process. Vessels can change hands frequently, thereby changing the insurance premiums as vessels are added and removed from the insurance coverage and requiring the annual reconciliation of their asset register for overall insurance risk exposure purposes. The first step was to digitize the vessel data, understanding both the current data and new data points that would be enabled by blockchain. In May 2018 a consortium including Ernst and Young, Microsoft, network security experts Guardtime, and insurers XL Catlin (now AXA XL, a division of AXA), MS Amlin, and Willis Towers Watson launched this blockchain solution based on the R3 Corda framework,[16] merging the existing digital data capture and transactions through smart contracts. At the time I spoke to XL Catlin's Digital Leader Hélène Stanway, and Ghanshyam Patil, Digital Lead for Blockchain, who explained more about the Insurwave project.

Patil told me that Corda was technically suitable because of the maturity of its smart contracts and validation processes and its capacity to scale the volume of stakeholders as the systems roll out to other insurers and fleets. The Corda framework is popular in financial services as a semitrusted network, and this suited the purposes of the consortium. Although insurers and brokers needed full transparency to keep their underwriting accurate, other parties had to be controlled by permissions. In a commercial market, it would be impractical to make insurance deals and premiums transparent, as each insurance decision takes account of multiple risk factors which would not be clear to third parties, and may result in disputes. The notary function, handled by Ernst and Young, provides the glue to keep the system churning. Stanway explained that the global asset register is held by the notary and smart contracts manage the insurance transactions when vessels are bought and sold. The system makes use of the IoT for prime entry to the ledger, and the sensors are delivering additional benefit by collecting more data points than could be captured or processed by the original system.

The proof of concept ran successfully during 2017 and Insurwave rolled out in May 2018. It has since widened its scope to include not just the hulls but each vessel's machinery and added a further piece to the jigsaw thanks to a partnership in May 2019 with China's Zhuhai port. There are also developments around interoperability with other blockchains: the vision of a global, joined up supply chain system cannot be achieved with siloed systems.

Another consideration is that if sensors are tracking the location of the hulls, then you could track the containers within them, and ultimately goods throughout their transit. Kuehne & Nagel's[17] existing Verified Gross Mass (VGM) portal already tracked the weight of loaded cargo to fulfill regulatory requirements, and in 2018, they incorporated a blockchain element for data verification and to provide transparency of shipment information. As data sets and records are combined over time, the picture of the cargos that cross our oceans will become clearer.

The Way We Work

Automation of back office services is not a new phenomenon. The humble spreadsheet was, until the arrival of VisiCalc[18] in 1978, a time-consuming job with paper, pencil, and eraser. This "first killer app" of the computer era changed finance roles forever, replacing a repetitive task with code and moving the focus of the accounting function from calculation to analysis and forecasting. There remains very little that is not in some way automated, with the possible exception of the manual sampling and checking processes of a traditional audit.

Finance and related functions may shun the limelight, but they are trailblazers in the use of emerging technology, pushing to make processes more secure, less prone to human error, and more reliable. We are seeing the use of artificial intelligence in fraud detection, data gathering from the connected devices and sensors of the IoT, forecasting based on smart data, and authentication of transactions through blockchain technology. The concepts of distributed ledgers and triple-entry bookkeeping come naturally to accountants, and finance and administration professionals have been quick to exploit this natural advantage in decentralizing processes. Significant advances have been made in the world of financial technology (fintech) around banking, escrow, securities administration, and audit transparency.

Decentralizing Finance

The traditional centralized banking system seems at first sight to be working perfectly well without a blockchain. Public perception of bank payments, particularly in a world where a tap of your smartphone to a sensor is becoming commonplace as a payment method, is one of simplicity and speed. Behind the scenes, however, it is a story of complex reconciliation of multiple accounts, administratively burdensome and entirely ledger based. If a payment is moving from one bank to another, there are immediately multiple parties involved in the transaction, and the cumbersome structure is a prime candidate for reworking in a distributed ledger. There is no reason why fiat currency could not be managed using a permissioned blockchain approach. There is no requirement to create cash, therefore no mining to be done, but the transfer of money and all related transactions can still be immutably recorded and confirmed by the distributed parties, that is the banks and the account holders.

A blockchain-based system powered by smart contracts can deliver greater transparency, confidence in the integrity of the records, and long-term cost savings into the bargain. Financial services and banking consultant Kapil Dhar told me that there is a huge amount of collaborative distributed ledger development going on under the radar across banking and financial services. Applications are being trialed at proof of concept scale in several areas as banks assess the decentralization use cases within their back-office functions. The expected benefits include potentially significant economies of scale and scope. The most mature projects have addressed cross-border payment applications, and adoption of the Ripple distributed ledger across banking in several countries worldwide is accelerating development. Ripple (using its XRP coin to effect transfers) and more recent competitor Stellar (using XLM), are fintech-specific technologies designed to manage cross-border payments. Some systems are live, including Santander's One Pay FX[19] app, which was the first blockchain-powered foreign exchange system to launch to consumers, released in the UK and several other countries in April 2018. In the securities market, ownership transfers are already being made using distributed ledgers. The first such transfer took place in March 2018 between Credit Suisse and ING,[20] and in April 2019 the Moroccan and Kuwaiti central securities depositories successfully piloted a cross-border securities settlement. The other priority for banking is work on digital identities to improve the Know Your Customer (KYC) process and combat money laundering operations.

Practical blockchain applications are emerging across several areas of financial services, and one institution, Northern Trust, has advanced blockchain technology with a series of U.S. patents.

Case Study: Northern Trust

In March 2018, Northern Trust deployed for its Guernsey-based private equity operation a set of new enhancements to its January 2017 release of its Private Equity Blockchain product, including a system whereby their auditors PwC, as well as KPMG, can directly access fund transactions, permitting real-time audit for private equity lifecycle events.[21] Anthony Stevens, Global Head of Product Innovation at Northern Trust, explained that the work began with onboarding clients and streamlining private equity lifecycle events, for example a capital call event using functionality developed using more "traditional" technologies. The blockchain aspect of the product development became important when interacting with firms who needed access to raw data that was a true golden copy of the fund's events, regulators and audit firms being good examples. The external parties can access nodes on the system and have developed technology that will provide alerts when specific data points are added to the node, enabling them to extract data as required. As a result of this simple innovation, the auditors reported a significant operational reduction for their work on the private equity accounts involved in the first rollout.

The underlying blockchain for private equity servicing took time to settle. The initial stack was built on Ethereum, moving to an IBM supported Hyperledger on the IBM cloud and eventually to Hyperledger's open source Fabric framework on the Azure cloud. The first live capital call was processed on the blockchain in 2017 with the fund managers including Emerald Technology Ventures processing multiple calls via the application from mid-2018 onward. The system reached a significant landmark for scalability in June 2019 when Northern Trust announced its transfer to Broadridge Financial Solutions.[22] The initial rollout expanded the platform's reach to the state of Delaware, where Broadridge are continuing to develop the system's functionality at scale. The aim of the transfer to Broadridge is to allow the full ecosystem to be developed at a much quicker pace, and for all parties involved in the Private Equity asset class to access the groundbreaking technology developed by Northern Trust.

The innovation at Northern Trust has continued. Stevens and his team turned their attention to some of the administrative headaches around their private equity business to see whether blockchain might provide a viable solution to some of their specific challenges. The first of these related to the new Economic Substance regulations[23] governing businesses domiciled on Guernsey. Registration in this British Crown Dependency, located just off the coast of France, has a number of benefits for certain financial organizations. The substance regulations were introduced in January 2019 to ensure that firms running funds on the island could prove to the local regulators that they were managing the funds in line with the local rules, provide transparency into the processes, and ensure that profits registered by businesses on the island reflected "economic activities and a substantial economic presence." This proof of economic substance included a requirement for directors to prove they were physically located on the island when voting on board and statutory matters, as evidence that a business was being properly directed and managed within the jurisdiction.

In a similar vein to Professor Mike Smith's solution when faced with Scandinavian regulators querying his client's data, Northern Trust developed a mobile voting app and collected GPS data from the directors' devices, hashing and timestamping both the location and the vote to the satisfaction of the local regulatory rules. In the all too common event that a director was genuinely unable to reach the island to vote, due to vacation or, more likely, a fog-bound airport, then proof of intent such as flight reservation and cancellation records were used in place of GPS data, so providing the required proof in case of a fund review.

The team then turned their attention to the legal agreements governing the management of private equity funds. Requirements for different funds can be complex because options around ethical investing or personal beliefs must be taken into account. The legal agreements surrounding the funds must identify any exclusions to be applied in individual cases. For example, one set of investor documentation may specify that there is no investment to be made in alcohol, or armaments, or companies domiciled in particular countries. This must be translated to the appropriate legalese and enforced in the management of the fund.

Working in partnership with tech startup Avvoka, part of an accelerator program within law firm Allen and Overy, Northern Trust developed the capability to deploy legal clauses as smart contracts directly from a digital legal agreement.[24] The Avvoka engine holds the template of a legal agreement, which can be parsed appropriately for the preferences of whichever law firm is acting for the client. The exclusion requirements are selected by a simple drag-and-drop from the smart contract library and incorporated in the legal agreement in the language required by the lawyers. This avoids forcing standard exclusion wording into complex documentation while retaining the underlying consistency of the smart contract. Once approved and signed, the agreement is recorded on-chain and the smart contract is generated direct from this document. This workflow avoids the challenge of encoding the detail of a legal agreement by turning the process around and starting from the needs of the developer.

The development of smart contracts for exclusionary purposes is ongoing: as clauses become more complex, automation must follow. For example, does the exclusion of investment into companies generating profits from alcohol apply purely to drinks companies, or to groups where just a small percentage of the revenue comes from this industry? There is also the question of making changes to smart contracts once they are incorporated in the blockchain, and here Northern Trust have been leading with field with a number of patents addressing this process. For example, the reappointment of auditors is an agenda point in a digital board meeting, and the result of the vote automatically triggers the extension or replacement of the appropriate smart contract and changes any permissions as required.

By focusing on the needs of a specific niche, this work has succeeded in demonstrating that blockchain can be applied successfully in audit processes. We will look more closely at challenges in the wider world of accounting and audit in Chapter 7. Northern Trust's work has also delivered tools that will be valuable in supply chain administration.

Collaboration in a Trustless Economy

Blockchain is gaining traction in business communities where there are links between key parties and a need to improve efficiency, transparency, and authenticity. It is also making an impact in fields where there is no trust relationship between parties at the same level of a hierarchy, but all of them have relevant inputs into a central point. They may be reluctant to share their information with competitors at the same level but must make it transparent to the party above. Blockchain technology has a role to play in overlaying confidential data repositories with a layer of encryption and enabling access for only those parties with the right key.

Medical records immediately come to mind as an area where this problem persists. Electronic health records are traditionally stored at provider level, which results in fragmentation and discontinuity across different databases. This is as true in a private health system such as the United States, where data is held separately by a range of providers, as in a public system such as the UK's National Health Service, where data is siloed within geographical NHS trusts. One of the earliest pilots addressing the complexity of patient records was launched at Beth Israel Deaconess Medical Centre in 2016 by MIT's MedRec project team.[25] The white paper proposed "a distributed access and validation system using the blockchain to replace centralized intermediaries." The MedRec system featured several mechanisms to link individual registry IDs to the system (the Registrar Contract), to link patients to each provider they had used (the Patient Provider Contract), and to form a breadcrumb trail for patients (the Summary Contract) linking back to their providers and serving as a backup allowing them to access or download their history at any time. The 2016 proof of concept for MedRec 1.0 was a success, and in order to scale the system beyond the original pilot and increase the security around medical records a new architecture was proposed for MedRec 2.0, which is under construction.

Case Study: Gospel Tech

The personal sensitivity of the data involved in health care means that the MedRec project is moving more slowly than some commercial applications of similar principles. London-based Gospel Tech has taken a comparable approach to solving a sensitive data sharing and collaboration problem for clients in the aviation industry. They explain the data paradox that led them to a blockchain-based solution:

> Traditional infrastructure means key data becomes centralized in silos, protected under more and more complex layers of security, which eventually degrade as employees circumvent protocols in order to collaborate. Ironically, this focus on preventing data from moving leaves enterprises more vulnerable to breach or loss of control of their data, whilst also restricting the true value of the data to the business.

The Gospel Data Platform helps companies and their supply chains to share sensitive data securely and confidently without exposing too much or the wrong information. Under the hood is a private permissioned blockchain using a Byzantine Fault Tolerance consensus mechanism (pBFT), which manages granular, authorized access to the information that's needed without compromising confidentiality. As Gospel explains, before their system was implemented one of their clients was managing parts traceability for aircraft across a wide supply chain by holding regular meetings to compare versions of spreadsheets. Now, all the relevant parties participate in a network of Gospel nodes with access to a single source of truth. The blockchain sits across a variety of supplier systems as an extension to each node's existing infrastructure, allowing users to sign in seamlessly and securely using their local credentials. The delay in parts traceability has fallen to minutes, improving overall efficiency and reducing costs.

Gospel's platform is also being used in the field of human resources and payroll processing to manage complex data flows between disparate systems. Speaking to *Computer Weekly* in April 2019,[26] the Chief Technology Officer of NGA HR, Stuart Curley, highlighted not only the simplicity and security of using the Gospel blockchain layer but also the importance of keeping immutable records of any changes made to the data. This theme of authentication, verification, and transparency runs through every successful blockchain implementation.

Managing the World Around Us

Widening the focus from the supply chain and back office functions, management of the infrastructure which surrounds us can also benefit from using blockchain and distributed ledgers. There are two areas where development is moving forwards rapidly: one the management of energy distribution, and the other addressing the full lifecycle of large capital projects.

Decentralized Energy

The supply of utilities to homes and businesses is complex and almost without exception centralized. This reflects the historical structure of provision of the resources that we consume. Energy is a case in point: for more than a century we have relied upon huge centralized power plants using fossil fuels, nuclear energy, hydroelectric dams, waste, and renewable sources. However, technology is advancing rapidly, and the generation of power is no longer truly centralized. Solar panels are appearing on rooftops across the globe. Factories are powered by their own forests of wind turbines. Why should the provision of electricity not become as decentralized as its production?

There is a real incentive for change in the energy market. Dale Geach, technology and innovation manager for Siemens Digital Grid,[27] told me that the market is under pressure to meet the energy needs of society in a sustainable, efficient, and resilient manner. This is the Energy Trilemma, and the solution lies in the transformational trends of digitalization of energy management and the move toward distributed systems.

As far back as 2016, a survey conducted by the German Energy Agency[28] revealed that almost three quarters of the decision makers who responded were aware of the potential impact of blockchain, 39 percent were planning implementations and 13 percent were already trialing innovations in the areas of peer-to-peer trading, charging of electric vehicles, and using blockchain for payment processes. In a 2019 paper reviewing the challenges and opportunities around blockchain in the energy sector,[29] researchers from Durham and Heriot-Watt universities working with Siemens Energy Management identified several areas where blockchain could improve current processes. These include consumer administration in billing, identity management, and even smart contract-driven provider switching mechanisms; smart grids, decentralized networks and data transfer; and disruption of wholesale energy markets. Within these, microgrids and consumer-centered marketplaces appear to be the closest to realization at scale.

Microgrids and the Rise of the Prosumer

As domestic renewable energy generation becomes commonplace, many households are simultaneously consumers and producers. These "prosumers" are distinct from commercial producers and passive consumers and are an essential node in the new breed of microgrid.

Microgrids have been in use for years: they do not by definition involve either renewable energy generation or decentralized administration. Engie[30] describes a microgrid as "an energy supply network built around local power and heat generation facilities. It is designed to operate autonomously or in synchronization with a national grid within a clearly defined area." The efficiency of a microgrid in remote locations has been established and tested over a long period of time, for example, the Hartley Bay microgrid in Canada was originally set up in 2008, predating both the Satoshi white paper and the mainstream adoption of renewables at a local or domestic scale.

The aim of the Hartley Bay project was to demonstrate advance metering and demand response,[31] one of the three significant developments in technology which are now enabling the evolution of microgrids around the world. As smart grids and smart metering roll out across existing the utility infrastructure, data collected on energy consumption becomes more granular and plentiful. This facilitates machine learning for prediction of consumption, aiding microgrid planning and design. Operationally, smart metering also enables accurate billing to be incorporated as an automatic function in the administration of a microgrid. The second key development is the increased efficiency of renewable energy technologies that put electricity generation within reach of homeowners, landlords, and businesses. Finally, the emergence of blockchain technology has provided the glue to connect the multiple independent participants in a microgrid network, and the transparency to discourage bad actors.

While established microgrids in remote communities rely on a centralized source of energy, a decentralized microgrid can draw energy from many unrelated sources for local distribution. A distributed ledger enables a microgrid to operate as a decentralized network, reducing costs and the administrative burden for both producers and consumers, and improving transparency and accountability. A fully functioning, decentralized microgrid will ultimately maintain the ledgers of individual generators, processing micropayments for kilowatts contributed to the overall grid.

As the 2050 deadline for a net zero carbon footprint is closer in capital project terms than we might think, the imperative for change is driving development. Energy innovators LO3[32] are behind a number of projects including the Brooklyn Microgrid (BMG) in New York, Enexa transactive energy in Australia, and the Allgau community energy project in Germany. Their original peer-to-peer energy trial in Brooklyn in 2016 involved five prosumers and five consumers and processed the first ever live energy transaction on a blockchain between a prosumer's smart meter wallet and the end consumer. The second phase scaled to include more than 300 homes and small businesses, and in 2019 BMG reached out to the wider community to launch its local renewable energy marketplace. The project is working to educate potential users in order to ensure smooth and informed adoption of the microgrid structure as it rolls out.

Let's now move from microgrids to macro scale and examine how major capital projects can benefit from the application of blockchain.

A Holistic Approach to the Capital Asset Lifecycle

Complex engineered assets such as offshore platforms, power stations, and process plants have a clearly defined lifecycle from design intent through construction, commissioning, and operation to decommissioning and recycling. The challenge of disposal is particularly critical because of the knowledge that is lost through the decades. How could this knowledge be preserved reliably throughout the asset lifecycle?

In 2003 four obsolete U.S. Reserve Fleet hulls, dubbed the "ghost ships," arrived on the British coast[33] to be dismantled by expert

reclamation operators. After a five-year delay due to environmental pro-
tests, the Able UK Environmental Reclamation and Recycling Centre in
Hartlepool finally started work to break up the vessels, dealing with pol-
lutants and recycling what they could of the materials. The Able UK yard,
which lies at the mouth of the river Tees, is still humming with activity.
It was responsible for breaking up the legendary French aircraft carrier,
the Clemenceau, and has regular business dismantling oil and gas drilling
platforms just a few miles from the docks where new rigs are being built.
Even though oil rigs return to the Tees like spawning salmon to the river
of their birth, there is a knowledge gap. Local legend tells of a 36" pipe on
one such platform whose purpose was lost in the mists of time and memory. What ran through that pipe? What pollutant should the breakers
account for? Is it safe to recycle the metal, or is it scrap? Without a ledger
of record valuable resources are being lost, as disposal becomes the least
risky option in the absence of certainty.

Teesside-based Kraken IM (Information Management) took on the
challenge of this complex supply chain, and now work with global oil and
gas giants to turn the existing system of record to a true ledger of record.
Their initial focus is on ensuring that all relevant information from individual manufacturers and contractors is available during construction and
is sufficient for commissioning and operation of a vessel, platform, power
station, or other major capital asset. This is a complex task: records must
cover everything from the supply of 10,000 fire extinguishers to the construction of process plant and must be of comparable quality across the
diverse range of pieces which make up the whole. As CEO Ian Cornwell
explained, a multibillion-dollar project may involve over a million individual items of equipment, and the data on each piece must include the
design intent, its function, materials, and operational information such as
maintenance manuals. There are a lot of competing systems of record and
teams that run them who hold this wealth of data, and as a result there is
often a need for a systems integrator to make sense of the patchwork. This
builds additional layers of cost and complexity and into already highly
complicated projects. Furthermore, data can be transferred across different systems during the decades of operation of a capital asset, with all
the additional costs and field matching challenges and failures that such
transfers always involve. It's a recipe for confusion and waste.

Kraken's vision is to move the industry from systems of record to a ledger of record, changing a document-centric industry to a data-centric culture. Cornwell gives the example of an aspect of a project where the design intent is "I need a pump just here." There will be engineering requirements, standards, and local regulatory constraints that impact on the specification against which suppliers will be asked to tender. A supplier may propose a slightly different material which in their experience will be more effective in the setting. Even before the pump is fitted, changes may have been made against the design intent. Recording the individual stages of approval ensures that at commissioning it is quite clear to the operator what has been supplied. This is a step toward greater clarity at the end of the lifecycle, where the asset can be dismantled based on the reality of what has been supplied, not the initial design documents. A full ledger of record for Architecture, Engineering, Construction, and Operation (AECO) would give a transparent asset history sufficient to maximize the recycling effort, creating a genuine circular economy for engineering equipment.

The Halcyon information management platform developed by Kraken initially focuses on approval milestones in the project lifecycle between supply and commissioning. The audit trail shows when an item was supplied, who supplied it, what it is, how it compares to the original design intent, and decisions affecting it through construction. This growing data corpus not only supports the asset lifecycle but gives greater scope for analysis and decision making than standalone documentary systems. There was one barrier to adoption that Kraken had to surmount: persuading engineers to let go of their documents, and to trust in the data instead. As Cornwell explained, "The only thing we cared about was the provenance. We already had an approval workflow but proving when something was signed off and what exactly it was opens doors to other functions."

Blockchain's transparent and immutable characteristics provided the solution. By anchoring the date, time, and approval details to a transaction on the Tierion Chainpoint network, they now had provenance for signoffs. They also achieved transparency for information that is not as static as a system of record might suggest. Decisions and planning throughout the project rely upon easily available data. For example, being able to define the weight of a unit made from many components is essential when planning the logistics of construction, such as hiring the right crane for the job.

One of the things that interested me was Kraken's experience of reliable prime entry to the ledger. Blockchain gives us trust in transactions but is not a repository of absolute truth. How could users be sure that the milestone was recorded accurately? According to Cornwell, the action of making the transaction visible to all parties has resulted in people being more conscientious about the entry itself. This is pleasingly reflective of the original concept of public announcement of a digital asset transaction, as outlined by Wei Dai in 1998 and adopted by Satoshi in the 2008 Bitcoin white paper: Visibility is an arbiter of trust. In addition, Kraken's clients have observed that the actual approval process has become more rigorous because of the immutable record that is generated. The engineering world is naturally risk-averse, especially when dealing with hazards such as oil, gas, and nuclear power. As accountability becomes more onerous, for example following the Hackitt Report[34] on London's 2017 Grenfell Tower disaster, parties who know they may have to stand by their decisions in an enquiry are very careful to do things right.

The Hackitt Report called for digital by default product specification and persistent identity for components, which is the ultimate goal for the AECO supply chain, and proposals went to public consultation in June 2019, which, if passed, will see persistent identity and traceability become law in the UK. Full equipment traceability has wide implications not only for safety but also to enable a decision-making shift from lowest initial capital expenditure to lowest total expenditure over an asset's lifecycle. This holistic approach to the capital asset lifecycle may lie some way in the future, but the building blocks are in place.

Enterprise Blockchain at Scale

The adoption of distributed ledgers in the private sector has moved reasonably quickly thanks to a combination of realistic problem-solving, talent coming into the sector in search of the next big thing, and development of underlying frameworks including the Hyperledger suite, IBM Blockchain, Ripple's early innovations in the fintech space, and spinouts from Ethereum.

The commercial imperatives surrounding the private sector have driven development predominantly toward permissioned blockchains. This fragmentation has been compared to stages in the adoption of the internet and World Wide Web by business: private intranets and bulletin boards were adopted before more open systems, and locally hosted servers are now gradually being superseded by cloud storage as infrastructure security improves and confidence increases. There are concerns around the long-term scalability of private blockchains, of which the most obvious is that in a blockchain without a native cryptocurrency, what are the appropriate mechanisms for trust once the network scales beyond known parties? This and other questions are already being addressed by developers at the coal face of distributed ledger evolution, and the next decade will be particularly interesting.

What could be achieved with blockchain technology in a world unconstrained by commercial sensitivities? Let's turn to developments which are emerging from a different source: the world of gaming.

CHAPTER 5

Digital Cats Will Change the World

On the 30th birthday of the World Wide Web, Tim Berners-Lee confirmed what we all secretly believed. Asked by journalist Samira Ahmed,[1] "Did you think there would be so many cats on the web?" Berners-Lee replied, "That was the plan all along, to fill the web with cat videos." Joking aside, the social aspect of the internet is something that was not immediately foreseen when the technology started to infiltrate our homes. The earliest use of the World Wide Web reflected our habits and activities at the time, making them arguably more efficient and accessible, but fundamentally unchanged. We sent e-mails or set up web pages instead of sending letters (in my case and for many others these did, in fairness, feature a reasonable volume of cat pictures). We gradually came to trust stores on the internet to take our credit card details and keep them safe and secure, moving shopping online. The rise of the cat video came from the new social constructs of MySpace, Facebook, Twitter, and the explosion of platforms that now surround us, and from the peer-to-peer file sharing which preceded peer-to-peer payments. Our behaviors changed because of the technology and would not have done so without it.

The Innovation Game

One of the dangers of enterprise-led innovation is an underlying requirement to maintain the successful business model. Following the principle of "if it ain't broke, don't fix it," even the most inventive companies can find themselves simply iterating for lower costs, or for the faster completion of existing processes which remain fundamentally unchanged. The risk associated with radical changes in behavior is sometimes too much for investors who are keen to realize a return in a short timescale. Return on investment can be difficult to quantify when technology is emerging. Project assessors will struggle to prove estimates of long-term cash inflows for traditional rate of return or net present value calculations. On the other hand, as we have seen, there is equal risk in innovation for its own sake. Some excellent ideas fall by the wayside when solutions are developed before clearly defining the problem. Workplace transformation is notoriously unsuccessful if it imposes new ways of working on unwilling subjects. If one end of the industry is hampered by risk aversion, and the other by overenthusiastic adoption of new technology regardless of its relevance, where can genuinely new concepts take hold and flourish?

There is one sector whose great strength is its imagination. Some of the most exciting innovation in the blockchain space is coming from the gaming industry. This is hardly a surprise: gaming has been at the root of other major shifts we have already experienced in the technological landscape. User interfaces such as touch screens and virtual, augmented and mixed reality were adopted in gaming before getting a foothold in the mainstream of enterprise. As one of the steppingstones leading to the development of the internet and World Wide Web, the multiplayer Empire game on the University of Illinois PLATO system is recalled fondly by Eugene Jarecki[2] who played it as a child growing up in the 1970s. The explosion of artificial intelligence in the 21st century owes much to gamers' demands for faster gameplay and more detailed graphics. Hardware stepped up to keep pace with the needs of a lucrative industry, and the new generation of graphics processing units (GPUs) produced for gaming also enabled the complex data analysis and algorithmic learning at the heart of artificial intelligence.

Gaming has inspired the development of concepts that could not have been otherwise realized without blockchain, and new behaviors are emerging which will have an impact upon the future of our everyday lives, at home and at work. Asset ownership has taken on a life of its own by using nonfungible tokens (NFTs) and their unique, indivisible properties to represent individual items. Where industry has been exploring the use of NFTs in asset twinning, gaming has taken the concept and run with it to introduce decentralized ownership and lay the foundations of a new and vibrant economy. At the same time, developers have had to address the challenge of capacity for the volume of transactions processed in a game and the amount of data that can be physically recorded on a blockchain. Games are remarkably complex when you break down the rules. Few of us realize how much processing we carry out internally when deciding on our next move. For effective automated gameplay there are hard decisions to be made about the value of each transaction and whether it is necessary to record everything on-chain, and the smart contracts governing each move must be highly efficient, costing gamers as little as possible in transaction fees and taking the minimum time to verify.

Gaming innovations are moving rapidly and have implications for business models and commercial behavior in the future. Let's look at them in more detail.

A Gaming Mindset

Ownership in a game is deceptive. When you have walked miles to catch or hatch a rare Pokémon, earned or paid good money to buy special outfits for characters in anything from Angry Birds to Fortnite, or mined the materials to construct your diamond castle, it feels as if you own something. You can compare Minecraft worlds with your friends and strut with pride in a multiplayer environment, but in reality 'your' assets remain firmly on the servers of the gaming company, or static in your licensed copy of the game. As Deckbound's Gareth Jenkins explained at the 2018 Blockchain Game Summit[3], gamers are ready for blockchain: it fits their mindset. They have an expectation of ownership of the assets they create and win during gameplay, including the ability to buy and sell items. Marketplaces already exist for the exchange of items in many role-playing games (RPGs), but the assets themselves do not belong to the players who are trading them. Shifting to a state where there is individual ownership feels like a natural step and opens new doors for gamers. Blockchain provides the medium in which this can be achieved.

This was part of the impetus behind long established gaming giant Atari's quest to create a token. Speaking to Atari Token cofounder Daniel Doll-Steinberg, we discussed the virtual world theory underpinning this and other developments in blockchain. Value in the real world is created through selling your skills, your time or your assets, and similar value could be created in the virtual world if games have the mechanisms in place to exercise the same economic and monetary principles. The skills honed through hours on a console are starting to deliver transferable real-world value at the highest level. We are seeing the rise of e-sports with the English e-soccer competition, the ePremier League (ePL)[4], and among the new generation of Formula 1 racing drivers, 19 year old Lando Norris ascribed some of his success and his ability to read other drivers on the track to his years of sim racing[5] and participation in the McLaren Shadow Esports competition. Even Fortnite has stepped into the arena with its 2019 World Cup Finals in New York streamed to millions of fans. However, deriving value directly within a gaming platform from skills, time or investment, rather than in a discrete competition, is an entirely new opportunity. If this can be harnessed—and blockchain offers the means to achieve it—the subsequent creation of value will kick-start a sustainable, democratized, worldwide economy. This is the disruptive vision of gaming which drives development in small, agile companies and which Atari has recognized.

The development of the Atari token has been a much slower and less public process than other more well-known blockchain game projects. As a NASDAQ listed company, Atari could not jump into the ICO space with the same agility as smaller enterprises and start-up companies, but their vision led them to plan for a token sale under complex NASDAQ regulations. Doll-Steinberg reflected on the pressures of developing a structure for the project where the founders were comfortable with the innovation environment while also meeting regulatory requirements. He recalls the frustration of watching some teams with little or no business experience raising money and failing fast while Atari Token's highly skilled founders were taking the long road. The more agile independent companies were liberal with public information about their plans, but Atari was bound by listed company restrictions on releasing anything which could affect their share price or breach stringent insider trading laws. The press picked up on the story thanks to a few lines in a mandatory report for the Paris Bourse in February 2018, but by this time the 2017 bull market had collapsed and the ICO gold rush was declining rapidly. Plans for an ICO were abandoned in the summer of 2018 but Atari have continued to invest internally.

The bulk of development in blockchain gaming has been focused on small companies. This is what we have come to expect with disruptive innovation. As the internet started to gain traction, existing market leaders failed to catch the wave, and Google from the garage and Facebook from the dorm overtook them. In gaming, the larger companies don't yet have an incentive to change their strategy. Their business models are profitable and sustainable, and they are in the same position as large enterprises across all sectors who are not ready or able to experiment and risk affecting their bottom line. When the tipping point comes, though, Atari at least will be ready to react.

What disruption is emerging right now from innovators unfettered by regulatory requirements? Value creation from ownership of digital assets has been the first source to be realized, and rewards for time invested and skills developed are not far behind. Let's now turn our attention to digital cats and see why they are going to change the world.

Cryptokitties and Nonfungible Tokens

If cat videos are the emblem of the modern World Wide Web, then digital cats are the flagbearers for the future of blockchain and cryptocurrency. When Cryptokitties[6], the first high-profile blockchain game, launched in November 2017 it immediately grabbed the attention of the blockchain community. Such a large volume of transactions was carried out on the Cryptokitties marketplace in the first few days after launch that the Ethereum network struggled to cope with the load[7]. This excitement was not due entirely to the fact that, at last, here was a fun outlet for your cryptocurrency. Sharp eyed developers reading the open source code realized that once you purchased your cartoon kitty, you had absolute ownership of this cute feline asset. Closer inspection confirmed that when you breed two kitties together you own the offspring, and that every kitty has a unique combination of traits inherited from its parents and defined by the smart contract that executes the breeding transaction. Every kitty's genetic code is recorded as a discrete digital asset using a *nonfungible token* (NFT). We touched on programmable money in Chapter 2: let's recap.

ERC 20, ERC 721, and ERC 1155 Tokens

A token is not simply proprietary cash but can be a measurement of value, a nonmonetary asset, or a degree of influence in a community. Most commercial applications based on the Ethereum Virtual Machine and incorporating their own native currency are using what is known as an ERC20 token. ERC stands for Ethereum Request for Comment and refers to the relevant discussion in the open source community which led to the development of each type of token. It is clear from the numbering that many proposals are discussed, but only a handful are viable and go on to be adopted by the developer community. ERC20 is digital cash: these tokens are often known as *alt coins* and they behave like money. All the tokens are the same and are divisible, much like a dollar bill. Thousands of ERC20 tokens have been created. Many have been used commercially for crowdfunding through ICOs, some retaining and gaining value as their related applications gain traction, and others worthless. Such tokens are often referred to as "shitcoins", and a valueless holding is known among investors as "dust". The majority of blockchain based games use Ether (ETH) directly for in-game purchases and actions, although a few have their own ERC20 currency built into reward and player retention mechanisms.

Gaming has harnessed two other ERC tokens with special properties. The Cryptokitties game and others like it have adopted ERC721 as their token of choice. ERC721 is a "one of a kind" token. They are still freely exchangeable, but each token's individual relative value will vary according to its specific characteristics, its uniqueness and rareness. In technical terminology, this means that the token is not "fungible". Fungibility is a property of currency whereby, for instance, any dollar bill can be used to buy a drink worth one dollar or less, with change making up the consistent exchange value. By contrast a nonfungible token (NFT) represents a unique, discrete item, a collectible which has its own value based on its own properties and the perception of the buyer.

It is quite simple to visualize an NFT in the context of Cryptokitties. Although all the cats have the same basic cartoon outline, every cat is slightly different thanks to the genetic traits ascribed to them. Some people find certain traits attractive and will assign subjective values to a cat with purple paws, or another driving a go-kart. They are also indivisible: you can't slice them up, as that would be cruel.

NFTs represent a groundbreaking concept which is transferring to other sectors outside the world of online gaming. What assets in the real world are unique and could be represented accurately and immutably in the parallel digital world? This is something that is being investigated by both the private and public sectors and will drive changes in provenance, investment, property ownership, asset twinning, and other applications.

The ERC1155 standard, finalized in June 2019, combines both fungible and nonfungible token types under a single banner. Championed by developers Enjin and supported by the wider Ethereum developer community, the token allows a single smart contract to manage different classes of asset within a game. As Enjin's Witek Radomski explains, in a fantasy role-playing game the fungible type is "useful for stackable items that don't need to be differentiated, like a bundle of arrows for a bow" whereas "a pet dragon… could be an NFT and have a unique name of its own, a power level, and a rich history in the game."[8]

Now that assets of all types can be owned, we start to see value creation from investment. Mechanisms in a wide variety of games allow collectors to enhance their kitties and improve their resale value, train their pet dragons for higher value and greater game success, or even rent out virtual land to other players. The value that players ascribe to assets is another aspect of the unique gaming mindset: investment in the game.

Paying for Play

It is immediately striking that gamers in the blockchain space are willing to pay to play. Every token must be purchased, or transaction fees paid to generate new tokens within game play (for example, when breeding new Cryptokitties). In a world where we have become used to getting things for free, this may seem a counterintuitive development, but the free model is not sustainable for economic success in the long term, as many platforms and publishing houses are belatedly discovering. Bringing a monetary culture back into the mainstream has positive implications both for rewarding creators and for the sustainability of an alternative economy. Crucially, it shifts the focus from spending purely for gaming enjoyment (paying for upgrades in a standard game, for instance) to potentially earning a return on the investment of time and money made in playing.

Cryptogames entrepreneur Gabby Dizon of Altitude Games defined three characteristics of gamers in the blockchain space when we spoke in May 2019.

Collectors are most interested in buying and holding some of the rarer NFTs in a game. They are the equivalent of real-world hobbyists, enjoying their collection and adding and divesting assets for pleasure as time goes on. They may well profit from their activity in the long term, but making money is not their primary motive.

Investors have a return firmly in mind. They want to make a profit from the portfolio of assets that they buy, or at the very least make enough to break even on their investment and then play without any further risk as fiat to crypto exchange values fluctuate. The return could come from straightforward buying and selling or equally from mechanisms in the game which generate income from the assets held. In Cryptokitties, owners can hire out their kitties for breeding and earn siring fees. In Axie Infinity, land parcels can be rented out, and there are similar gameplay constructs in most emerging blockchain games.

Players will include people in both of these other groups but cover a much wider spectrum, from high-school kids through to seasoned gamers who simply play for the fun of it. Any earnings from their investment in the game come as a bonus. These are the people who are more likely to start creating value through their gaming skillset and the time they spend on a platform. As e-sports have started gaining traction and value, so we can expect the top players of fantasy games and RPGs to have an opportunity to develop online careers. The implications for the future of work are staggering.

It is vital to the emerging game economy that there is a balance between these different types of users. When a game launches, the investors and collectors are the first to engage, but it is the regular play and volume of activity among the community of gamers that determines the success of the platform and the returns to be made.

Cryptokitties, as the first game to hit the headlines, is fundamentally a collecting game. The smart contracts that govern the genetic code in generation after generation of cats reveal rare traits and incentivize owners to continue breeding and buying to increase the value of their portfolio.

The game suits the collectors and investors who seek long- and short-term returns on their ETH purchases—and there is money to be made. Shortly after launch, one kitty sold for 253 ETH, and in September 2018 another was purchased for 600 ETH,[9] although these figures are unusually high.

The static collectables format is unlikely to hold the attention of hardened gamers in the long term. Hard on the heels of simple structures like Cryptokitties and Gods Unchained we start to see games coming through which combine the ownership of NFTs with active gameplay, for example Axie Infinity, which features collectable characters, battles between teams, breeding of new Axies, and land ownership and management, or the groundbreaking Neon District. Bringing such complexity onto the blockchain requires and inspires even greater innovation in terms of ease of access, scaling, transaction processing, and overall user experience. We will address these challenges later in this chapter: for now, let's look at the final piece of the jigsaw for successful game development.

The Importance of Community

Social media started to change our communication habits from around 2008 onward, and enterprises in multiple sectors have homed in on community engagement as a key marketing tool. Community management is a new but important discipline for holding the attention and loyalty of consumers. Advertising practice has shifted over the decades along a continuum from "telling"—one-way communication on billboards, in print and on broadcast media—through interaction between the enterprise and the customer, to "listening," which encompasses everything from review sites to semantic and sentiment analysis of social media posts. Good community practice takes this one step further, creating a networked structure with layers of engagement, which holds the interest of consumers or employees and makes them feel a valued part of the whole. Achieving a truly mature community made up of diverse individuals is often difficult. The Community Roundtable's maturity model[10] defines the expected development stages of a successful community and is based on a large body of research on engagement and management strategies stretching back to the earliest days of corporate intranets.

According to the Community Roundtable's annual research, members of a community range from a minority of eager contributors to a silent majority of listeners and lurkers. On average, one in 10 members of a community will actually be engaged in the day-to-day discussions, and the holy grail of community management is that the activity of the network holds the attention of the core while drawing the lurkers into the discussion. It's a tough job in the noisy world we inhabit with so many different platforms and social groups competing for our attention. My own daily round includes Facebook feeds and groups, Twitter, LinkedIn, and Instagram, multiple Slack channels, WhatsApp chats, Telegram groups, and Discord, and I cannot follow all the discussions. Asking people to engage in yet another medium can be met with everything from disinterest to hostility. The bottom line, though, is that communities form most naturally around a common interest and a need. Gaming has a head start on enterprise, with mutually supportive groups clustering around games from the earliest days of standing together in arcades through to the Steem, Reddit, and Discord groups that exist online today.

Community is an essential aspect of blockchain and cryptocurrency adoption. Where an enterprise chooses to use ICO crowdfunding, the first community that must be built is that of investors and collectors who have the wherewithal to support fundraising for development. They must have ready money, trust, and patience. Once the funding round is complete, the established community needs to evolve in order to attract and engage potential users who will generate anticipation and excitement for the launch. This is true for all enterprises regardless of sector: the engagement effort does not stand still once funding is in place. Once launched, new users of any decentralized application will find themselves in a new and potentially complex environment where there is no central authority to pick up the pieces in case of a mistake, and the support of their peers is vital. When this need for community support is combined with the gaming culture of cooperation around the interpretation of complex rules, there is a great resource for gaming companies to listen, react, and refine their offering.

Gabby Dizon reinforces the impact this has. "Creating a game economy from scratch needs a strong player community," he told me. Not only is community important within the context of a single game, but also for building engagement with the players of other games. Nothing develops in a vacuum, and interoperability and collaboration are vital in building interest, excitement, and ultimately engagement with each new game as it launches. Dizon and other leaders in blockchain gaming have a vision of meta-events across platforms, leveraging the power of community to enhance, not compete. This is something which is enabled for the first time by sovereign ownership of assets through the mechanism of NFTs.

Nifty Moves

Outright ownership of game assets using nonfungible tokens is a groundbreaking concept because it represents something that could not be done without blockchain technology. At first sight it seems to be a simple nice-to-have feature which can take buying and selling activity outside the game platform, but what else could you do with your NFTs? Gamers may wish to take the asset and use it in another game: to be fair, a cute cat in a two-dimensional cartoon may not be useful on a Call of Duty battlefield, but how about a fully tooled-up Overwatch character?

The way an NFT is represented across applications differs according to the environment, but ownership is undisputed. A token could be listed in an inventory application, used as a basis for bonuses and rewards, or even act as collateral for borrowing. Coming back to the economic and monetary principles of the virtual world, here we have the mechanism for value creation from skills, time, and assets. Tokens can be programmed in a way that physical assets cannot, and managing interoperability opens more doors. NFTs have some very nifty moves.

Interoperability of Nonfungible Tokens

Cryptokitties creators Dapper Labs took the first step into the unknown through their 2019 partnership with a different game, Gods Unchained. Each Cryptokitty token generated a limited-edition card pack in Gods Unchained, and fancy Gods Unchained cats appeared in Cryptokitties.[11] The interoperability of tokens in a collaborative ecosystem is yet another feature peculiar to blockchain technology. These cartoon cats are leading the way toward trustless co-ordination and cooperation between proprietary systems across multiple sectors, not simply in gaming. Rather than using APIs to bring assets in from different sources, NFTs could move between systems independently, subject to formalities such as intellectual property rights on design elements. What other assets could be represented, recorded, exchanged, or licensed in a decentralized structure? We have already seen in Chapter 4 that work is underway toward establishing a persistent identity for assets and equipment in capital projects, and some companies are exploring the use of tokens to represent each unit, unique by serial number or physical characteristics. The aspect of using digital assets as a financial security also merits closer scrutiny: they have intrinsic value and ownership is clear. This is a new way of thinking and may represent a behavioral shift to come.

Intellectual Property and Asset Ownership

One of the considerations for enterprises using NFTs in their application is protecting their intellectual property. Cryptokitties founders spent time working through the pros and cons of NFT ownership, and eventually published the Nifty License.[12] This recognizes the company's ownership of the generic cartoon style of the cryptokitties but grants to the owner of each token broad rights to use the cartoon with that token's unique markings and features. The Nifty License is a way of linking the physical and the virtual: when challenged, the owner of the digital asset can authenticate their rights to use the related imagery. Released for use by any developer, this license is a blueprint for collaborative creators who don't want to lock down their work but still need to retain some control and set up a path to monetization.

It seems logical that the principles behind the Nifty License and the ability to encode the metadata of a unique asset into an NFT could be applied to sectors outside gaming. In music, artist Imogen Heap has developed Mycelia for Music, a research and development hub for music makers. Part of the Mycelia mission is to ensure that all artists are "paid and acknowledged fully" for their part in any work. This is especially relevant to the music industry where tracks are commonly sampled and incorporated into other works. Most such activity is above board, but lawsuits for music plagiarism have been part of the landscape for decades. The Mycelia Creative Passport was launched in 2019, and the Grammys blog[13] reported on Imogen Heap's plan to protect music makers by giving them "proper credit, digitally." However, researchers from the University of Ulster, in a report commissioned by the UK's Intellectual Property Office, sound a note of caution.[14] They acknowledge that "blockchain looks like a partial solution to ease the strictures of the royalty framework" but recognize the complexities of the industry and the wide range of activities in the music value chain. The report identifies a number of projects at varying stages of development and adoption who are all tackling different aspects of the industry's challenges. These include include the aforementioned Mycelia; the Ujo project from ConsenSys; the Musicoin[15] streaming platform; dotBlockchain, a partner of Intel, whose mission is to eradicate losses from rightsholder information as file types change; and Custos, whose copyright protection system and Interplanetary File System (IPFS) are attracting considerable interest for musical content tracking and attribution. As in our global commercial supply chains, there are many pieces of the jigsaw coming together.

In those supply chains, too, there are plenty of uses for an NFT. The Durian fruit producers we met in Chapter 4 are identifying each unique fruit and encoding its metadata in an NFT for tracking all the way to the consumer. California-based Centrifuge are addressing a different problem in the supply chain using the same methodology, allowing financial business documents to be created as NFTs. Ultimately, the technology that arrived in the mainstream as a digital cat is now representing a wide range of assets across the world.

Scaling the Blockchain

In every game there are clear rules governing each move that a player makes. Consider straightforward board games such as Othello, or checkers, or Connect4, before even thinking of the variations in chess or go. Every move involves knowing the way that pieces are permitted to act and thinking ahead and calculating the potential outcomes. When you consider the complexity of the reasoning involved, you see why games have been the training ground of artificial intelligence from Deep Blue to Deep Mind.

Once a move has been made, by human or AI, we can write this action to a blockchain so that it can be authenticated by other parties.

But could we go further? It has already been established that smart contracts on a distributed ledger enable the execution of transactions. Coins are transferred from one wallet to another, registry entries are created for shares and property, life events are written to identity records, and a Cryptokitty with a unique ancestry-derived genetic code can be created. Surely a move in a game is a simple smart contract? It seems logical that blockchain can become the referee, checking that the move made is legal and the outcome correct.

Of course, there is a catch. Take a simple game like Connect4. There is only one possible move: a colored disk is dropped into the frame as two players attempt to make an unbroken line of four in any direction. What is required to confirm that the move is valid and to check whether a player has won on that move? The smart contract would need to establish:

1. Is there exactly one more disk in the game than at the end of the previous move?
2. In the additional disk of a different color to the one previously played?
3. Has a line of four been formed horizontally, and / or:
4. Has a line of four been formed vertically, and / or:
5. Has a line of four been formed diagonally?

To verify this simple move there are several functions, each with a cost. As the complexity of a game grows, the gas fees for smart contract processing would be eye-watering, to say nothing of the energy burden of data processing, the wait for validation, and the overwhelming noise of all these entries rendered immutably on the blockchain.

Addressing the challenge of scaling is critical in both gaming and wider enterprise blockchain and essential for bringing the speed and throughput of cryptocurrency transactions to the standard of existing centralized payment processors. There are numerous solutions emerging across many different protocols, all at varying stages of development. These complement wider work in both technology and software design, which is needed to bring blockchain and cryptocurrency into the mainstream at large scale.

Scalability and Speed

When blockchain was first introduced as the technology underpinning digital cash, the ultimate vision was of a global decentralized payment system. Thanks to the development of electronic payment processing by banks, the Visa system, and private mechanisms such as PayPal, the first thing most people think of when they consider the processing of a high volume of transactions are the twin metrics of speed and throughput. How fast does the blockchain propagate, that is, how quickly is each new block created, and how many transactions are processed on each block? One measure of this is how many transactions per second (TPS) can be achieved.

In terms of throughput, global mainstream processor Visa reports that in 2018 it processed 124.3 billion transactions on its networks for 3.3 billion card carrying consumers.[16] This is approaching 4,000 TPS at a vast scale. PayPal, whose 267 million active users made 10 billion transactions in the same period,[17] comes out at approximately 317 TPS. By contrast, Bitcoin trundles along at a sedentary seven. Successive cryptocurrencies have bettered this, and although a few have reported throughput close to Visa levels this has not been tested at the scale and vast capacity of established centralized systems. Ethereum reportedly reaches up to 30 TPS and Litecoin closer to 50 TPS. The fastest established crypto payment processor is Ripple with around 1,500 TPS for the XRP coin, although as this is achieved through the Ripple protocol consensus algorithm and not on a public blockchain it may not be a valid comparison. The all-time high for EOS, according to the EOS Network monitor, is 3996 TPS, but day-to-day live transactions run at a fraction of this figure, showing under 100 TPS when accessed in August 2019. EOS has been designed for high scalability in a deliberate effort to stand shoulder to shoulder with Visa, but the structure of the EOS blockchain and its delegated Proof of Stake consensus mechanism result in a more centralized structure than traditional cryptocurrencies.

How can transactions per second be increased? In basic terms, this involves either increasing the number of transactions that can be completed each time a new block is generated, or the speed with which the blocks propagate, or both. Of course, it is not so simple. In Chapter 2 we addressed the introduction of Segregated Witness (SegWit) to the Bitcoin blockchain, which changed the structure of the block contents, and the disputes over block size, which led to successive forks of the chain into Bitcoin Cash and its derivatives.

Transaction speed, or latency, is a different side of the scalability equation. According to the Kraken cryptocurrency exchange, the actual time taken to move a coin from one wallet to another varies across a broad range from the near-instant Ripple and Stellar to a full hour for a Bitcoin payment. A significant part of the speed equation is the consensus mechanism used by each blockchain. Proof of Work is pure but slow. Any attempt to speed this up, for instance by making the mining algorithm easier, compromises the security of the blockchain. The Ripple protocol consensus algorithm, the EOS delegated Proof of Stake consensus, and Stellar's federated Byzantine agreement system (FBA) are all examples of effective, fast mechanisms, but there are concerns over centralization where validator numbers are limited. This suggests that there is a trade-off between true decentralization and transaction throughput.

How will the speed and volume of processing grow? New blockchains are being developed with speed and scalability in mind. There are plenty of teams waiting in the wings and reporting test processing at hundreds of thousands of transactions per second. The market is skeptical of many of these claims simply because showing fast processing on a test net and a limited network of servers is very different to transactions in the real world. However, there are some exciting projects underway. Among these is Algorand, launched in July 2019, which has attracted a lot of attention with its platform claiming a throughput of 1000 TPS and a five-second latency at a test volume of half a million transactions. It uses a new Byzantine Agreement protocol for consensus by committee with verifiable random functions to select the user who will propagate the next block as the chain grows.[18]

Sharding

The Ethereum network is considering a concept known as sharding. This is used in traditional database management where large data repositories can be partitioned for faster processing. It is used for huge databases where users would otherwise be waiting a long time to retrieve their information from one source: multiple data shards speed up the process. Search engines, large e-commerce sites, and CRM systems all use sharding techniques. The parallels with the needs of blockchain are clear. The Ethereum sharding project aims to split validation workloads among different groups of miners, breaking the whole blockchain into shards or microchains carrying only a fraction of the transaction data. Since the nodes would no longer need to process each and every transaction, this can theoretically increase the speed and throughput of the network. There are complexities to be addressed with sharding, not least in security, ensuring that a particular shard cannot be compromised. However, randomizing the allocation of each shard and changing nodes regularly is one solution.

Ethereum is not the only protocol looking at sharding. It is also of interest to Hyperledger, and some new blockchain projects are adopting sharding structures from the outset. As the concept has been proven in centralized databases, it is only a matter of time before the additional considerations for implementation in a decentralized setting are resolved. However, for the existing blockchain ecosystem, simple linear scaling is not going to put Bitcoin on a par with Visa, and sharding may not be the answer to every question.

Let the Side Chain Take the Strain

Bitcoin, Ethereum, and other truly decentralized blockchains run on what is known as a "gossip" protocol. This means that every transaction is broadcast to every node. This is one of the great strengths of the technology but as transaction volume grows, there are no easy economies of scale to be found. Developers are working on solutions that sit alongside the established system without compromising its structure. One of the most straightforward approaches to scaling has been the development of side chains as a second layer on the established protocols.

Side chains were first proposed in a 2014 paper by Back et al.,[19] which introduced the concept of "pegged sidechains." It suggests the "transfer [of] an asset from the (original) parent chain to a sidechain, possibly onward to another sidechain, and eventually back to the parent chain, preserving the original asset." These side chains, the authors continue, would be independent blockchains and as such could host innovative development and experimentation. It is a concept that has been adopted and taken forward successfully by several developer groups. Let's look at the innovations around the Lightning Network on Bitcoin and the gamer's favorite, the Loom Network.

Lightning Network

The first generation of live side chain projects began with the Lightning Network on the Bitcoin protocol. In their 2016 paper,[20] authors Joseph Poon and Thaddeus Dryja proposed "scalable off-chain instant payments" for the Bitcoin blockchain. The authors recognized that as every change in state of the Bitcoin ledger is broadcast across the network, this could never be scaled to compete with the centralized payment systems currently servicing the world's commerce. They proposed that transactions could be processed in separate channels with only the final change of state being broadcast. This decongests the network and reduces the costs to the user as fees are only payable to miners when the change of state transaction is processed on the main blockchain.

A good example of how this works in real life is simple day-to-day micropayments. Want to buy your coffee in Bitcoin? Waiting for validation and confirmation from the network means a long line and cold coffee. Instead, such micropayments can be managed through a Lightning Network app. You set up a small balance in Bitcoin, much like a prepay debit card, and buy your coffee using this balance. At any point, either when you no longer need this one-to-one link to your vendor, or at a point in time such as the end of a month, the change of state, not the individual transactions which led to it, can be written back to the blockchain. In accounting terms, which are a good analogy, the side chain holds individual journal entries for each coffee purchase in a ledger account, and the Bitcoin blockchain shows only the opening and closing balances of that account at a point in time.

Lighting Network developers have addressed a number of security concerns, including how to manage disputes about the account balance on a side chain without compromising the main blockchain record. Lightning has inspired a wave of side chain innovation.

Plasma

Plasma is a development layer on Ethereum with a similar goal to sharding, but a structure not dissimilar to that of Lightning. It enables the creation of "child" chains with their own distinct properties, which use the
main Ethereum blockchain as the trusted source. Special smart contracts
on Ethereum known as "root contracts" contain the rules that govern the
behavior of each child chain. Plasma is still in development as a standalone solution, but it has been adopted to reinforce asset security in the
Loom Network.

Loom Network

How do you deliver a decentralized gaming experience without slowing
to a crawl? The answer, according to the Loom Network, is to develop
application-specific side chains.

Loom's software development kit (SDK) was designed to help
non-blockchain developers to build the blockchain element of their systems in a straightforward fashion. Loom's team is also behind Crypto
Zombies, the definitive smart contract coding tutorial for those who want
to dig deeper into development skills. The SDK allows the construction
of a "DAppChain" sitting as a Layer 2 on top of a number of existing
blockchain protocols in the same way that the Lightning Network is a
Layer 2 on Bitcoin. The team behind Loom are aiming for it to become
the universal Layer 2 connecting all major current and future blockchains.
This is a significant step toward the seamless collaboration and interoperability that we have enjoyed for decades with the mature internet, and
Loom integrations are in place for Ethereum, EOS, Tron, and Cosmos
among others.

Increasingly popular with developers of games, Loom is also used for
social networks and other applications that require speed and high levels
of user interaction. The default SDK uses Delegated Proof of Stake consensus for all the individual side chains, although developers could choose
other mechanisms, and this means that transactions on the side chain
incur no gas fees and have the fast confirmation time that a Proof of Work
blockchain lacks. Compare this with applications native to Ethereum,

such as Cryptokitties, which incur fees for every transaction and take time to validate. Launching a game on a side chain enables the use of highly complex smart contracts for gameplay. The first DAppChain went live in March 2018 and Loom is used by several growing games including Axie Infinity, Battle Racers, and Neon District.

Loom has adopted Plasma as a method for users to transfer ERC20 and ERC721 tokens onto sidechains with the knowledge that should there be any problems with the sidechain, such as a hack or fraudulent activity, that their assets are still recorded on the main Ethereum block-chain. This bolsters the security of side chains and makes them a realistic and reliable platform for scalable development.

Practical Considerations for Scaling Blockchain Projects

Speed is not by any means the only measure of a successful system. There are plenty of other factors to consider, not least a loaded question asked by Blockchain Game Alliance's Alex Amsel: Do you need to scale if you don't have users? As we have seen before, having the "best" tech-nology does not guarantee that that market will follow. Competitors on slower frameworks could easily win greater market share, and there is nothing to be gained by future proofing an application which has no users.

If the system features any type of interoperability, it should remain in the same blockchain ecosystem as its collaborators: this is one of the strengths of Loom in widening collaboration networks. Software develop-ment kits (SDKs) vary in their thoroughness across frameworks, and the more support that is available for technical teams the greater the integrity of the eventual platform. Anyone seeking a new, faster option needs to look carefully at the team behind the development, doing the due dili-gence that is required with any early stage business.

Add Just a Pinch of Blockchain

Software developers using blockchain can meet all these scalability efforts halfway by reducing on-chain processing. Amsel takes the view that if something does not have value (whether monetary, commercial, or personal) then it does not need to be on a blockchain. This is a good rule of thumb to follow in developing sustainable applications.

Take an objective look at the processes that are being automated. Be honest about what elements of the user journey really require an immutable, distributed record to be created. There will be considerations beyond simple functionality and authentication. Businesses often rely upon valuable data as a commodity, therefore broadcasting even meta-data to a network can compromise the business model. An example of the way blockchain has been used to good effect for this type of business is the Gospel Data Platform discussed in Chapter 4: the introduction of a distributed ledger has been carefully managed to solve a problem while protecting the data which participating businesses hold and value. If there is a genuine business reason to incorporate complex smart contracts into the software, then the next step is to consider the needs of both the users and the developers.

Focus on the User

It is all too easy as a software developer to lose sight of the user and focus instead on the technology, pushing to have the cleanest processing, the fastest validation, the best experience from the very particular point of view of a developer. Users are not generally concerned what is running under the hood. They want the software to execute the functions for which it is designed through a straightforward user interface with suit-able security and resilience. In the past, when running a growing soft-ware business, I learned to spot the innocent statement "just refactoring something..." This normally flagged up a developer falling too far down the rabbit hole into a wonderland of new tools, and future proofing far beyond the roadmapped scope or needs of the product. Designing for the expected growth in users according to a realistic business model is important; chasing the fastest blockchain experience at the expense of a good user experience and proven resilience is foolhardy.

Marguerite deCourcelle, CEO of Blockade Games, is clear that blockchain developers need the complementary expertise of application developers to achieve good user experience. She points out that, "when Epic Games made Fortnite, they simultaneously developed the Unreal

Engine to power it. They made development choices in real time based on the requirements for the gaming application." It is the high-quality user experience that drives adoption and access to a mainstream user base. Blockade, the company behind Neon District, released their blockchain game developer platform in September 2019 as a tool for the industry to achieve this collaboration. It turns the process on its head: established game developers can use the platform to build in blockchain features which will enhance their application. The goal is to make it so that players don't realize they are playing a blockchain game. This frictionless adoption is something that every industry should strive to achieve.

CHAPTER 6

Government, Governance, Data, and You

Where is your data, exactly? Do you know how it has been folded, sorted, sold, and abused since you signed up for that useful free internet tool? How much of your private life has slipped into the public domain through innocent games and chat online? They say that McDonalds may not have the best burgers in the world, but their real estate portfolio is second to none. The business of the company you subscribe to is not based on providing you with a free service, but on selling your details directly or indirectly to a hungry market. If the product is free, then you are the product.

Scandals over data breaches, misuse of our personal information, and increasingly complex regulation have brought the topic into sharp focus for individuals, corporations, regulators, and governments. The safe management of data concerns everyone, and as blockchain technology gains traction there are opportunities and threats to address on all sides. The opportunities lie broadly in the arena of authentication without knowledge, transparency for multiple unrelated parties, and process efficiency. It offers individuals a way to decentralize their data and to take ownership of their personal information and is also a useful tool for security by design in centralized organizations. The corresponding threats appear in the shifting sands of regulation and a need for developers themselves to be extremely diligent in deploying accurate code and building up intellectual property. Blockchain (as distinct from cryptocurrencies and tokens, whose regulatory environment was discussed in Chapter 3) requires careful consideration in the context of regulation. There are significant challenges for developers and innovators who must navigate the minefield of differing privacy laws across multiple states and simultaneously manage the protection of their own commercial interests and intellectual property.

This chapter addresses the journey toward owning our data, the implementation of blockchain in areas of government, and legal considerations for any organization adopting distributed ledger technology.

Value Your Data

We have become accustomed to having information about our personal lives stored digitally and often publicly. Zip code finders, telephone directories, and electoral rolls were among the first public repositories of data on the internet. These held much the same information that we once could have retrieved on microfiche and paper from our local libraries but made it available to a vast new audience whose motives for its use may not have been straightforward. As privacy awareness grew, these lists were hidden from public view. Social media gathered pace in the early 2000s and we began to share our data voluntarily, posting everything from baby scans to holiday plans for our friends and family to see. The rise of online services and connected devices through the IoT has triggered a third wave of unconscious data sharing. As Avast security ambassador and former world chess champion Garry Kasparov says, "The Soviets had spy devices: now we just pay Amazon to deliver our data."

Privacy Versus Surveillance

We are living in a world where our personal privacy is traded off against the utility we derive from services. We are advised to make conscious decisions on data sharing, but sometimes the choice of whether or not to share data is academic if we want to access essential services. To complicate matters, every individual has a different level of tolerance across four different elements of privacy as defined by Alan Westin in his 1967 book *Privacy and Freedom*: solitude, anonymity, reserve, and intimacy. These behaviors are easy to see on social media, where some users share every detail of their lives, uncaring or unknowing of the risks they run in doing so. Others are more reserved, sharing cautiously, and still more crave absolute anonymity, hiding behind pseudonyms and choosing their platforms according to the level of detail that is required to participate. There is also a historical and well-documented conflict between privacy and surveillance. The fallout from Edward Snowden's 2013 whistleblowing over NSA surveillance programs and the PRISM and Upstream initiatives were far-reaching, damaging trans-Atlantic relations over privacy and throwing the activity of the security services into the spotlight. On the other hand, the United Kingdom's GCHQ reportedly blocked around 2,000 malicious domains a week in 2018[1] and its surveillance of internet activity has helped to reduce terrorist threats and the activities of offender communities. We cannot have it both ways. As a society, we have a duty to protect the vulnerable, at the cost of absolute privacy.

Why has this become such a complex issue? In 1999 David Brin addressed the growing problem and proposed a solution in his book *The Transparent Society*,[2] which resonates with the subsequent development of distributed ledgers. He explains that prior to our collective submersion in all things digital, transactions relied upon personal trust and community transparency. You knew who the reliable characters were in your village, town, or market sector and adjusted your personal privacy settings accordingly. Equally, bad actors were controlled by the knowledge that dishonesty had a cost in terms of reputation and privilege in a small community. As the scope of transactions widened to include unknown participants in regional and national communities and across borders, secrecy in the form of encryption replaced the natural order of trust. However, our blind reliance on encryption being used effectively by a centralized data collector is dangerous. It is becoming increasingly easy to crack the layers of security around our data thanks to inventive hacking, social engineering, and phishing, and there are too many instances where human error or downright carelessness has resulted in data being collected and stored without appropriate encryption being applied—or, more worryingly, any encryption at all. Data theft is a growing problem as the information held on us becomes more valuable than the costs of stealing it, despite considerable efforts on the part of lawmakers to curb the wilder excesses of unnecessary data capture and commercialization of our personal information. As the volume of stored data grows, we must look to other solutions for protection. What Bitcoin, blockchain, and discussions of security and regulation have brought to the fore is a reimagining of transparency and trust online.

Digital Identity

According to many observers, the holy grail of technology is digital identity. The ID2020 Alliance further states that this should adhere to the core principles of portability, persistence, privacy, and user control. Work toward developing a reliable digital identity has been going on since long before the advent of blockchain, but the distributed ledger has added a decentralized authentication layer to the mix. The Estonian government was the first to use cryptography and distributed records to protect the details of all their citizens. In 2003 cryptographers Ahto Buldas and Märt Saarepera developed a formal security proof for digital identity[3] and along with Mike Gault and Joichi Ito formed the Guardtime company when work on the e-Estonia program began in earnest around 2007. The goal of the researchers was to remove the need for a trusted third party in the management of identity, and they fell upon the same system of cryptographic verification via digital signature, hashing, and timestamping that also featured in Satoshi Nakamoto's Bitcoin whitepaper. The similarity of approach and the apparently coincidental timing of Buldas, Saarepera, and Gault's work has led to speculation that this group of developers could be candidates for the real identities behind the pseudonymous Satoshi, but they have not invited attention and Gault has denied any involvement when questioned. Guardtime has grown to be a multinational leader in blockchain innovation and was also involved in the Insurwave development discussed in Chapter 4. From digital identity, the Estonian government and Guardtime have moved on to the digital management of health care, residency, taxes, voting, and governance, incorporating blockchain technology where appropriate.

The United Nations is not far behind Estonia in its work toward the identity aspect of its Sustainable Development goals, to "provide legal identity to all, including birth registration, by 2030." They formed the ID2020 Alliance[4] in partnership with some of the largest digital providers on the planet including Microsoft, Accenture,[5] Cisco, and others. ID2020 aims to provide digital identities for some of the 1.1 billion unregistered people in the world using biometrics and blockchain, and is an extension of the existing biometric identity management system developed by Accenture and used by the UN High Commissioner for

Refugees. In 2018, pilot projects were run in Thailand in collaboration with the International Rescue Committee (IRC) for refugees accessing health care and building records of their education and professional skills, and in Indonesia with the National Team for the Acceleration of Poverty Reduction to improve access to energy subsidies for economically disadvantaged individuals. In a separate initiative the World Food Programme[6] implemented a private blockchain to overcome two administrative headaches in an existing food aid distribution system in a Jordanian refugee camp. Their goal was to protect the full identity of refugees by making this data a step removed from day-to-day authentication processes, and to streamline the complex administration of the retailer accounts and refugee aid allowances. They succeeded in protecting the details of 100,000 refugees by enabling iris scans as their means of identity and holding only that metadata on chain. As a bonus, the proof of concept implementation saved $40,000 a month in bank transaction fees, administration costs and the prevention of fraud.

Of course, identity is a concern for enterprise as well as government: in financial services, the need to Know Your Customer (KYC) is moving toward authentication from immutable, trusted records. In July 2019, a number of banks in the United Arab Emirates formed a blockchain KYC consortium for corporate identities[7] and in France in 2018 a pilot project run by 26 firms and five banks[8] demonstrated that repetitive, duplicative KYC processes could be streamlined through access to a common blockchain for authentication. If this nut can be cracked, KYC is the use case that will drive the adoption of digital identity in our comfortable first world.

Protecting Ourselves

Beyond identity verification, blockchain is a tool that can be and is being used to record, verify, and keep safe many other aspects of personal data. We can construct an audit trail of the essentials in our daily lives through the simple mechanism of timestamping, rendering the details we choose to record both verifiable and unquestionable when it matters. Just because we can, however, doesn't always mean that we should. We have gotten ourselves into enough trouble recording our lives on social media, so what benefit is there to having some of that information available for all time?

The answer, of course, is that if a problem arises which appears unsurmountable, it's worth looking at blockchain as part of a range of available emerging technologies to see where the right solution lies. Several entrepreneurs are working on solving very specific problems around the verification of personal data.

Anne Ahola Ward watched the surge in blockchain projects which focused on tools for the blockchain itself, solutions where there were no real problems, and lofty ideas that failed to deliver the nuanced detail promised in long white papers. Very little that she saw emerging was designed to help people or had been made easily accessible for mainstream users. The lightbulb moment for Ward, in the aftermath of family tragedy, was realizing that there is a point where it actually makes sense for your assets to be digital and owned: upon death.

Most people of Anne's and my generation have dealt with the estates of family members. There are challenges on all sides. Disputes arise over the most trivial of assets and the will of the deceased may be out of date by decades. Where there are active social media accounts there is no consistency of approach. On some platforms including Facebook, the option exists to memorialize a loved one's profile, but others hang in the ether, subject to the vagaries of changing terms and conditions, or may be lost permanently when a service shuts down. One of the most simple but overwhelming losses is the wealth of oral history which passes down the generations. Ward's vision is to use blockchain to protect a timestamped legacy, and the Veritoken Legacy Locket, launched in June 2019, starts with the upload of pictures, quotes, and memories, and is designed to record personal data choices and preferences. The new role of technical executor is a response to the new needs of those who remain. In the long term, keeping a legal will up to date may fall to the blockchain rather than to will attorneys. "We're not going to live forever," says Ward, "but our information can, so we should have power over that."

Another initiative focusing on a specific life challenge is the Loly dating app. Speaking to founder Adryenn Ashley, this app written by women, for women, addresses a number of problems that have not been solved by other platforms and for which blockchain offers a solution. It introduces trusted user identities supported by a mechanism for building reputation through community verification and reports of good dating behavior. It meets the need for clear recorded consent or refusal during dates that can be authenticated after the fact. Ashley also reports that the roadmap includes a safe word for activating emergency calling and recording functions.

The blockchain layer in these applications is not obvious to users, which is important for adoption of such tools on their merits, not for their technology. We may be moving to a world where we can own our data and manage our privacy and our identity, but the experience must be seamless and the technology usable by all.

Governing and Governance

Government and blockchain has been described as a match made in heaven. The gradual digitization of our public services has steadily transformed our lives and, despite the challenges of deploying complex software at scale, the process has been relatively painless for most people. Blockchain has emerged as one of several useful tools in the work to streamline public services, manage registries, and protect identity. In Estonia, the use of cryptography in digital identity predates Satoshi by several years, and the introduction of distributed ledgers has been a natural evolution. In Wyoming, legislators were quick to recognize the potential of the technology and the need for good practice around it. They have started to build blockchain solutions into several areas of government and business and also drafted and passed a series of bills that have been adopted by other states. In the United Arab Emirates, Dubai has incorporated blockchain into its long-term Smart Dubai project, aiming for a paperless administration. Let's look in more detail at the work underway in regulating for blockchain, managing registries, managing cities and citizens, and securing the democratic process.

Wyoming: the Blockchain State

The State of Wyoming is a trailblazer in blockchain regulation. Concerted efforts by the Wyoming Blockchain Coalition, including legislator Tyler Lindholm and Wall Street veteran Caitlin Long, enabled Wyoming to become the first U.S. state to provide a comprehensive legal framework for blockchain technology to flourish and benefit both individuals and companies. Several states have since adopted the same legislation. Within this suite of bills, enacted in 2018, Wyoming introduced a legal framework for digital assets. It ensures that the state recognizes direct property rights for owners of assets of all types,[9] classifying them within existing laws and frameworks as intangible personal property (whether money, securities, or other assets). Land, property, shares, and securities all have their registries, and with the rise of digital assets it is logical to expect these to also benefit from formal registry structures.

Land on the Blockchain

The traditional management of asset registries has been fundamentally unchanged for generations. Where once the register was written in ink and copperplate, it has moved to computerized databases and through different software platforms, coding languages, physical storage media, and prime entry sources. Registries are on one hand a ledger of transactions, and on the other hand a specialized archive with the same authentication and verification challenges as the National Archives detailed in the case study in Chapter 4. Transfers of ownership from one party to another, or from one party to multiple owners, must be reflected accurately.

Why is blockchain relevant to these long-standing systems? Until recently, improving efficiency and reducing both costs and the opportunity for human error in the management of the archive and the ledger could have be achieved with internal robotic process automation (RPA). The registries are generally held by a single party, so decentralization may not appear to be an immediate advantage. However, the process of monitoring, updating, and validating registries is increasingly decentralized. Changes of ownership, background checks, and interrogation of the register are more likely to be processed by third parties. As a public record, there are multiple parties involved in updating the details held on the register and any individual referring to the records must have confidence in the accuracy of the inputs. Blockchain not only provides a route to achieving greater efficiency at lower cost, but also improves the update process for transactions originating with third parties such as lawyers and makes the information more accessible and trustworthy. Land registries across the world rushed to test the concept of blockchain as soon as the potential benefits became apparent. There have been land registry pilots and proofs of concept running on every continent in countries including (but not limited to) the Republic of Georgia, Sweden, the United Kingdom, New South Wales in Australia, the state of Wyoming, Honduras, Ghana, Haryana in India (as part of a United Nations initiative), and Dubai. A handful among these have made the leap to live deployment, although others are still testing their platforms or have stalled altogether.

The economic incentives for the development of efficient and accurate land registries are clear: "Land rights are essential to promote economic growth, address economic inequalities, alleviate conflict management, and support local governance processes," say Benbunan-Fich and Castellanos in their 2018 paper[10] presented to the Thirty Ninth International Conference on Information Systems. Their contrasting case studies of the projects in Honduras and the Republic of Georgia demonstrate one of the real challenges of blockchain implementation. The technology is complex, and while the use case may be ideal and the solution theoretically viable, the information systems readiness in a public organization can be the difference between success and failure. Honduras was an early adopter, starting its digitalization pilot in 2015 in partnership with Factom, an experienced blockchain developer headquartered in Austin, Texas. Despite this promising start the project stalled within a year, unable to move at private sector pace and coinciding with the start of a politically charged election season.

At the opposite extreme, Georgia, independent since 1991, had already put firm processes in place for the management of their registries and embraced the world of blockchain through benefits for bitcoin miners and partnerships with BitFury. When it came to digitization, their National Agency of Public Registry (NAPR) was "information systems ready". The Republic of Georgia's blockchain registry was the first in the world to be deployed live and at scale. Mariam Turashvili, head of project management at the NAPR, confirmed to me that as at July 2019 they had "more than 2 million extracts from the public registry (hashes of ownership certificates) stored on blockchain" and were actively working on the smart contracts for processing transfers of ownership and other transactions, and the legislative amendments required to implement them.

Sweden's Lantmäteriet was one of the first public authorities in the world to move its land registry from paper to digital records, as far back as the 1970s, but technology has moved on since this time. The authority realized that the delay between any change of status or ownership and the entry on the register was compromising the transparency and trust placed in it. The delays were directly due to a heavy (and costly) manual system of signed documents, and the lack of transparency resulted from firewalls and security systems designed to protect the data but simultaneously blocking access to anyone without high level permission to write to the database. The advent of blockchain appeared to offer a solution to both challenges, and a two-year proof of concept exercise was completed in March 2018. This is not the only example of emerging technology being use in problem solving at Lantmäteriet. Natural language processing, handwritten text analysis, and artificial intelligence have been developed to improve their response to citizen requests for existing records. Blockchain is just one of many tools being used by a historically forward-thinking authority to improve its services.

Some of the most interesting early stage development is emerging in Africa. Bitland in Ghana, a Swiss partnership in Rwanda, and Land LayBy in Kenya are responding to endemic problems of fake title deeds and lack of consistent documentation. Although these are a long way from delivering a live and adopted system, they demonstrate a local response to the problem that is likely to be far more suitable and sustainable than anything imposed from outside Africa.

Although registries have been held out as one of the most obvious applications for blockchain technology, their development at scale is a slow process. The public sector is naturally cautious about the deployment of any IT system because people do not have a choice whether to use it, while the private sector races ahead, secure in the knowledge that competition in the market weeds out the weaker propositions. Land registries may have suffered from a period of hype, but the steady progress of landmark projects is likely to deliver real benefits worldwide in the next few years.

Smart Cities, Smart Lives

Land registries may be moving online, but what about our homes? This logical step in public administration also offers benefits to the real estate industry. The commercial incentive to reduce costs and improve efficiency has driven development in the private sector. California-based real estate platform Propy executed the first proof of concept property purchase on the Ethereum blockchain in October 2017, an apartment in Kiev, Ukraine, and has moved quickly to commercialize its offering. The first transaction recorded in California took place in July 2018,[11] and in Europe a few months later.[12] By the middle of 2019, Propy had over 60,000 properties listed and had managed sales in Bitcoin, Ether, and fiat currency in the United States, Europe, and Asia. The smart contract governing each transaction is triggered by an independent notary verifying the seller's signature, a much simpler interaction than the traditional exchange of documents. Propy is also trialing a deed registry and a title registry to manage the sale process from end to end. This weaves into the public registry by adding the hash information to the publicly held deed at the relevant Recording Office. The building blocks are in place for public and private sector collaboration.

Transactions don't stop with land and property. In 1999 the city of Dubai launched its ICT strategy with the aim of making the lives of its citizens happy and their interactions with government and regulators seamless. In 2016, a new element was added to the strategy: blockchain.[13] Sustaining a consistent long-term vision at state level and executing it over more than two decades is rare in the west, and the rapid progress of Smart Dubai demonstrates the value of planning outside party politics. The Dubai government took the view that "Blockchain will do for transactions what the internet did for information" and set to identifying the transactions that could be made frictionless in their citizen journeys. Their practical approach was not to use blockchain regardless, but to solve specific pain points with the appropriate technology. The strategy addresses three pillars: government efficiency, industry creation, and international leadership. Speaking at the Business Blockchain Summit during London Tech Week 2019, Dr Sohail Munir, adviser on emerging technologies and digital transformation to the Smart Dubai Government, explained that the goal is for the city to become paperless by December 12, 2021(there is a celebration already planned). The city envisages the elimination of 9.57 million pieces of paper, and cost savings annually of AED 1.15 billion (approximately $0.3 billion). This is an ambitious plan impacting multiple areas of a citizen's daily life, and it is on track to be delivered. At the time of writing, payment reconciliations and the city's property registry are already deployed, with proof of concept systems in place for aspects of licensing, wills, vehicle management, and education.

The government machine in most countries has a need for increased accountability and transparency, which could be delivered by appropriate application of blockchain. The long-term project for the digitization of Dubai's government and administration is one example. In the United Kingdom, blockchain as a tool for process improvement is being reviewed by the Department of Work and Pensions, the Intellectual Property Office, and the G-Cloud procurement system among others. The Canadian government published their Policy on Service and Digital in August 2019[14] with a specific commitment to "innovate and experiment with new technologies and solutions, like Artificial Intelligence and Blockchain." Advances in blockchain technology rely upon support at the highest levels, and government interest in developing the use of distributed ledger technology can only speed up adoption.

Trust in Elections

Blockchain technology is an essential tool in the development of internet voting and the elimination of electoral fraud. As our lives move inexorably online, maintaining an engaged electorate becomes essential to democracy. If voting is too burdensome, relying on paper and ancient machines, then citizens will be disenfranchised. However, electronic voting is fraught with risk and is far more complex than might be evident to the voter.

Professor Steve Schneider, director of the University of Surrey's cybersecurity center, explained to me that while tallying votes transparently is reasonably simple, transparency of individual votes is a different matter. A robust and verifiable voting system needs to deal with the eligibility and the anonymity of voters, maintain secrecy in the ballot, and demonstrate integrity. It is a considerable challenge in terms both of cryptography and cybersecurity. Writing for the *New Statesman* in May 2019,[15] Schneider outlined potential threats to both the electorate and electoral bodies including spoof voting sites, malware on devices used to cast a vote, and system penetration or internal bad actors, particularly as an electronic system is likely to be managed by a single central administration.

Academics have been working on electronic voting systems since before the advent of blockchain, developing ways for individuals to verify independently that their vote has indeed been counted as intended, and for the public to check that the votes have been tallied correctly. Pilots such as the Verifiable Classroom Voting (VCV) system[16] developed by Professor Feng Hao of Warwick University, and Schneider's own past work, originally relied on posting results to a bulletin board, but as Schneider told me, blockchain delivered the technology to make this public record immutable and fully distributed. There are caveats. The blockchain needs to be permissioned rather than public, as electoral authorities have to run the election according to the laws of the country involved. There is a need for a two-stage consensus to ensure that voters get an immediate confirmation that their vote has been cast and recorded correctly: waiting for a Proof of Work consensus on a public blockchain would simply take too long to be practical. Trials of the Surrey team's Verify My Vote (VMV) system[17] took place in summer 2019, and while this work is a giant step toward a transparent and verifiable electronic voting system, it is likely to be some years before this is mature enough for a political or statutory election. Schneider suggests, though, that we are getting closer to using it for less high consequence elections where the voter list is under tighter control (e.g., organizational elections, union elections etc.) and the risk/benefit calculation is different.

There are elements of internet voting systems in place already around the world. Digital identities are used in Estonia to ensure that all those eligible to vote can do so while maintaining anonymity in relation to the votes cast. In turn the votes themselves can be recorded in an immutable form. Estonia's electoral commission monitors the centralized system closely for tampering, but there is no independent verifiability in place as yet. A voting system which mimics Estonia's approach was implemented internally by a Danish political party in 2014, and there is a project in progress through the Bitcoin Foundation to develop a blockchain-based voting system.[18]

In West Virginia, the Secretary of State's office identified that for active service personnel the existing postal and electronic ballot systems

were not accessible.[19] The state ran a pilot program enabling 150 overseas voters to participate in the November 2018 midterm election using
the Voatz mobile blockchain application.[20] The city of Denver also tested
Voatz in its May 2019 municipal election for 4,000 eligible active-duty
military and overseas voters. In both cases election officials reported an
increased turnout in the small sample. It is important to note that Voatz
is a private company, not a government or academic-led initiative. The
system is likely to be tallying votes rather than offering individual verifiability, but there has been criticism of a lack of independent scrutiny.
Such reticence is unusual in the blockchain world, where the spirit of
collaboration and open source development generally reflects the transparency of the technology. It does however demonstrate one of the challenges facing businesses working to advance applications of blockchain
technology: protection of intellectual property.

Challenges for Blockchain Development

This book is intended for business decision makers who want to understand the landscape of blockchain and cryptocurrency, not for the developers who are likely to be following this fast-moving world of software
through online communities and collaborative projects. However, execu-
tives must be aware of the underlying implications for system design and
security in any new development in order to ask the right questions of
their technical delivery team.

Automation of processes can be fraught with problems. One only
has to look at the delays and complaints surrounding the launch of any
public service software platform to realize the complexity and the itera-
tive nature of automation. Changes to centralized systems of record can
be managed by the data owners, but what about decentralized systems
of ledger? When a process is automated and immutable, the smart contract that executes each transaction must be watertight from the outset.
In Chapter 2 we addressed the problems that can arise through errors in
deploying smart contracts. Code that controls transactions on the blockchain must be subject to much more rigorous testing and auditing than
centralized software. Day-to-day considerations including the management of intellectual property and the protection of data must also be

taken into account when solving wicked business problems and delivering smart user tools.

Branding and Intellectual Property

Who owns your website? The tangle of intellectual property, copyright, and open source materials that make up the average internet site is extraordinary. Taking a simple WordPress site, the code beneath WordPress is open source, with a large community of contributors and an open source license whose requirements must be considered when using or adapting the software. The icons and design of WordPress assets, such as the brand logo, belong to that company and there is likely to be a trademark registration in one or more countries. Your own logo may be similarly protected. The theme, which lies on top of the site and gives it its look and feel, could be an open source skin, or may have been designed by a third party who licenses its use to you, although they have no rights over your brand colors and logo. The words that you write for each page are likely to be your copyright. The images that you put on the page may be available on a creative commons license, or a paid license from an agency, or taken by you. If the picture is of an artwork, the copyright lies with the artist, not the photographer. So, who owns your website again? Where does the intellectual capital lie?

Professor Tonya Evans, Associate Dean of Academic Affairs and Director of Blockchain Law Online Certificate Program at UNH School of Law, says that intellectual capital is the most important asset of a business, but likely the least understood. Enterprises must take account of copyright in words, images or code, patents and trademarks, and trade secrets, and balance the business value with the wider needs of the market and consumers. The Cryptokitties team, in developing the Nifty license described in Chapter 5, retained their clear ownership of the cartoon style of their cats, while granting the use of each unique kitty design to the relevant token holder. This maximizes the intellectual capital for the creators, who need something to show for their work, and takes a sensible approach to the habits of online appropriation of images.

Open source collaboration in the development of blockchain is a major feature of the rapid innovation we have seen in the sector.

Evans reminds us that there are always restrictions around an open source license. When code is adapted from open sources, there could be some intellectual capital to claim on those adaptations. However, as criticism of Voatz (aforementioned) has shown, holding your cards too close to your chest can backfire in public perception. Retaining trade secrets must add value to the business. If secrecy detracts from the perception of the enterprise, it could be more damaging.

The other side of the coin is the value of blockchain to your brand. It is unsurprising that many businesses have sprung up with "blockchain" in their names, as this appears to differentiate them from the competition. It is equally unfortunate that a good proportion have not lived up to the hype. Now that the market is settling and hollow projects are falling away, it is time to leverage the good things about blockchain. Speaking at SXSW in Austin in March 2019, Shontavia Johnson, Associate Vice President for Academic Partnerships and Innovation at Clemson University, considered the features of blockchain that can be used to build a brand: customer trust, efficiency, and the ability to use apps to bring communities and influencers together around your brand. Leveraging a buzzword may give short-term gains but aligning your brand with the values and principles around the appropriate use of blockchain and backing it with action has long term value. Removing the jargon and demonstrating transparency, authenticity, credibility, community, and efficiency is a worthwhile business strategy.

Data Protection

Data protection legislation is a modern extension of the privacy laws that have evolved very differently across multiple jurisdictions in the last 150 years. In the United States, privacy laws developed through the natural evolution of common law, against the background of the right to free speech and freedom of the press, as enshrined in the Constitution and the First Amendment. While the common law tort of Invasion of Privacy grants the individual "full protection in person and in property," it has been applied through history on a case-by-case basis, and as both society and technology have developed the legislation has been trying to keep up with new contexts of privacy. In 1890, the target was the emerging technology of photography, which had resulted in some instances of over-aggressive journalism. "The Right to Privacy" by Warren and Brandeis, published in the *Harvard Law Review*,[21] remains an influential text and the concerns raised are recognizable in our modern society. Modern tort law, evolving since Warren and Brandeis, protects from "intrusion of solitude, public disclosure of public facts, false light, and appropriation." Federal law places limits on government intrusion, while individual states have added other protection piecemeal. This complexity of legislation has resulted in a patchwork of laws and regulations that can sometimes overlap or contradict one another. In the digital arena, for example, the California Consumer Privacy Act 2018 (CCPA) and the Biometric Information Privacy Act 2008 in Illinois are independent and unrelated pieces of legislation addressing very specific elements of privacy. Developers have a challenge to ensure that the data their systems are designed to capture and retain will pass muster under a variety of different laws.

The situation is further complicated by the cross-border adoption of software. Blockchain inspires a vision of a connected, decentralized world, but this requires conforming operations in different jurisdictions. Four letters strike fear into the heart of all tech firms: GDPR. The General Data Protection Regulations, which took effect across Europe in 2018, are onerous and have specific implications for immutable records in distributed ledgers.

How did European legislation develop in this way? In Europe, something is private unless declared otherwise, while in the U.S. privacy is an inalienable right, but invasion of such privacy is defined sector by sector and case by case. The difference can be traced to one major historical event and its legacy: The Second World War. After the war, the Council of Europe was formed, and in 1949 work began to develop the European Convention on Human Rights (ECHR), a very strong declaration in favor of democracy, freedom, and the rights of the individual. In 2009, the European Charter of Fundamental Rights combined the ECHR and individual pieces of legislation from different states into one Charter, which is legally binding on all states in the European Union. The right to personal privacy is explicit. This blanket protection is the starting point for regulation in Europe, with subsequent case law allowing limited access to personal data. The General Data Protection Regulations emerged from this background, restricting the actual collection of personal data unless this is done for a specific reason or, failing that, is collected with "informed consent," which is a complex minefield.

Case Study: SDQ

Professor Mike Smith is based in Europe and the Strengths and Difficulties Questionnaire (SDQ) he operates is being used worldwide. Mental health assessment, particularly with children, is a very sensitive area, and Smith's experience offers insights into the care developers should be taking over data capture and retention. He explains that he has always avoided collecting any demographic data. For completeness it is important to capture age and gender, which are relevant in the assessment, but these will not result in personal identification in a data set of multiple records. However, the precise date of birth of a subject is not collected because this could very easily be traced to one individual given other contextual information about the sample.

Although SDQ is unwilling to collect personal details, these are essential in a medical setting because clinicians cannot risk attaching data to the wrong patient. The solution to this problem requires blockchain and is permissible under GDPR because it is an example of security by design. It is a powerful mechanism for data protection.

Data is concealed by strong encryption and tokenization, rendering the stored information unintelligible in a manner that would take years for a bad actor to reconstruct. The unique ID of this data can be bound to patient information at the clinical side, local to the medical professional, and the stored information for that ID can only be decrypted by the keyholder. Each transmission of data is timestamped, providing an access audit trail for the unique ID but without knowledge of the contents. This protects SDQ by keeping track of the opaque "blobs" of data, proving that the information is still stored and has not been lost or maliciously deleted. Although this structure prevents a bad actor with partial information from accessing the stored data, there are considerations around custodianship of private keys: if a key is lost then valuable data is lost with it and cannot be retrieved. Solving this challenge once again falls to developers, to ensure that the security of data is not compromised by measures to protect decryption tools.

Looking to the Future

While enterprises can move quickly to meet challenges, and game developers follow their imaginations to break barriers, the path of innovation for government and governance is necessarily slower. The management of our personal data, our lives, and of nation states is not a straightforward task but the public sector is rising to the challenge and adopting new technologies more rapidly than we have seen in the past. Blockchain technology can enable some fundamental changes to the way we live, and it is refreshing to see so much innovation emerging from a traditionally slow sector. While many of the applications are not yet deployed at scale, the fact that they are live and being trialed and scrutinized bodes well for future adoption.

In our final chapter, let's turn to some of the as yet unrealized opportunities around blockchain, and the threats that lie ahead.

CHAPTER 7

Looking to the Future

The impact of blockchain and cryptocurrency on our futures will be disruptive in ways we cannot yet imagine, and distributed ledgers will be disrupted in turn by other technologies. We can expect our workplaces and family lives to change, influenced by a whole range of emerging sectors from artificial intelligence to mixed realities and a connected world alongside decentralized applications. There are areas where we can already see the opportunity for blockchain to disrupt systems and change lives, but the challenges of implementation have pushed the dream a few years into the future. There are also threats on the horizon that developers are already addressing: one of the timeliest questions is around the sustainability of the technology.

Is Bitcoin Killing the Planet?

The energy required to maintain blockchains is phenomenal. According to the Bitcoin Energy Index,[1] electricity consumption for the Bitcoin blockchain alone has doubled year on year, and in 2019 its annual consumption stood at over 73 Terawatt Hours. This is around the same energy requirement as the whole of Austria and takes no account of the load from the Ethereum network or any other public blockchain that relies upon Proof of Work number-crunching for its validation. Does the blockchain use too much energy? Andreas M. Antonopoulos, speaking at a Scottish Blockchain event in Edinburgh in June 2019, was clear: as a scarce resource, Bitcoin is using exactly as much energy as the market says it should. However, in this era of accelerating climate change, is the Bitcoin community acting responsibly?

Sustainable Proof of Work

The financial incentive for miners of any Proof of Work cryptocurrency is vital to maintaining the integrity of the chain. As a reminder of the process, in order to randomly confirm one block of transactions and open the next, full nodes on the Bitcoin blockchain compete to solve a complex equation. The first to determine the nonce value x, which will generate a hash value with n leading zeros for the block contents including the nonce, wins the race and is rewarded with the transaction fees and minted Bitcoin. This is a complex calculation with a high degree of difficulty, but it is worthwhile for miners to participate, and herein lies the first redeeming feature of the structure. Miners are not only incentivized to maintain the blockchain but to do so as efficiently as possible for their own commercial interests. As Harald Vranken points out in his 2017 paper[2] "Bitcoin miners initially used general-purpose computers, but they quickly switched to more dedicated hardware that offered higher performance … at lower energy costs." The efficiency of processors has continued to rise rapidly while the relative cost falls. This is not due solely to the need for high processing capacity in blockchain, although some suppliers have tailored their cards to solve the Bitcoin algorithm (Application Specific Integrated Circuits). Faster processing is related to the much greater demand for detailed, high volume data analysis in the world of machine learning and artificial intelligence.

The source of the energy used by these processors is a major consideration for the sustainability of blockchain. According to research published by the Coinshares network[3] in June 2019, three quarters of mining activity is powered by green energy. "We calculate a conservative estimate of the renewables penetration in the energy mix powering the Bitcoin mining network at 74.1%, making Bitcoin mining more renewables-driven than almost every other large-scale industry in the world," say the authors. This figure represents a slight reduction from the November 2018 analysis: use of renewables is an established method of reducing cost and mitigating climate impact, and the mix of miners shifts over time. Mining activity uses solar and wind power across the globe and has been seen to cluster near "relatively sparsely populated, hilly or mountainous regions traversed by powerful rivers" to take advantage of cheap hydroelectric power. Some miners and developers are also choosing their locations around the globe to minimize energy consumption in server cooling. In countries close to the Arctic circle, miners are using the naturally cool local climate to keep their servers at operational temperatures and substantially reduce the need for air conditioning units to run at full power day and night.

The march toward renewables is not always a welcome strategy. Existing renewable generation companies are fighting back against miners flocking to cheap energy hotspots[4] such as the cities around Niagara Falls which have since banned miners from operating. However, the Coinshares research concludes that the wider economic impact is in fact beneficial. "Bitcoin mining is acting as a global electricity buyer of last resort and therefore tends to cluster around comparatively under-utilized renewables infrastructure. This could help turn loss making renewables projects profitable and in time—as the industry matures and settles as permanent in the public eye—could act as a driver of new renewables developments in locations that were previously uneconomical."

This is not a universal opinion. Research undertaken by Peter de Vries of PwC dives deeper into claims of Bitcoin's sustainability.[5] Although the degree to which renewables are used is undisputed, de Vries highlights the fact that a mining processor has a constant demand for energy from the moment it is switched on to the point at which it degrades sufficiently for its operation to be unprofitable. This consistent demand for energy is at odds with the variable nature of renewable energy supplies, placing pressure on other sources including, for example, coal-fired power stations in the mining-heavy Sichuan province of China. He goes as far as to suggest that the energy requirement is such that it may require the construction of new power stations in the region. The advances in Proof of Work processor efficiency are also a concern, says de Vries. Processors wired to solve a single algorithm cannot be repurposed at obsolescence, resulting in substantial electronic waste.

Initiatives to harness renewable energy, increase the efficiency of processors, and manage their recycling and reuse are still essential and the concerns raised by de Vries must be addressed alongside these strategies. Achieving sustainability for Bitcoin and other Proof of Work coins is a huge challenge, which can only become more onerous as cryptocurrency scales, and is further complicated by the use of blockchain technology beyond crypto.

Is There Always a Need for Blockchain?

Proof of Work is not the only energy guzzler on the horizon. It is the nature of a distributed ledger to be, well, distributed. Every party to the ledger has a copy stored locally. In a centralized system, the database is held in several locations for security and users read the data through API links to the relevant software interface. In a decentralized system, there could be hundreds, thousands, or even millions of copies of the same data requiring more storage and more processing power to keep the ledger state up to date on each node.

Blockchains for both crypto and commercial purposes are being gradually streamlined to reduce the amount of data held on-chain. The impetus for this is improvement of the user experience by making transactions confirm more quickly, but the reduced pressure on the blockchain in terms of processing and storage of data contributes to the overall sustainability of the technology. Bitcoin, for example, started work on its Lightning Network in 2015 and the community continues to refine it. Lightning adds a layer of individual peer-to-peer channels where microtransactions can be processed with only the final balance of a channel being immutably timestamped in the blockchain. These initiatives are contributing to more efficient and therefore more sustainable processing in the long term.

Equally important is the use of sound judgment on what applications are suited to a blockchain. If a system is working perfectly well using a centralized database, if there are no requirements for a third party to authenticate records, if only a single organization is writing to the database, then there is no reason to jump to a new technology for the sake of it. Enterprises must use emerging technology effectively and ethically, whether this involves development of artificial intelligence, smart devices, autonomous vehicles, or blockchain applications. Loading many nodes with data that could be as easily held on one is wasteful of resources, and very little benefit can be derived. As we saw in Chapter 4, blockchain is effective when it solves a problem. If there is no problem to solve, then there is no value in shoehorning a solution into a working business model just because you can. However, blockchain has the potential to change lives. The World Economic Forum[6] has estimated that the technology could stimulate a trillion dollars of trade from underdeveloped countries and small businesses. The work being done to improve blockchain and cryptocurrency sustainability is vital to ensure that these benefits do not come at the cost of accelerated climate change.

While Bitcoin will always retain its Proof of Work consensus, there is a lot of work underway to find behaviorally sound and Byzantine Fault Tolerant substitutes for this elegant, effective, power-hungry consensus mechanism. In Chapter 2 we looked at both different consensus mechanisms in detail and established that reducing energy consumption on a blockchain through adoption of Stake and Authority mechanisms may require a permanent trade-off against the relevant cryptocurrency's independence from a central authority. This is an area that is constantly evolving, and the optimal energy-efficient consensus mechanism for an open, neutral, borderless, decentralized cryptocurrency may still be some years away.

Threats to Blockchain Integrity

The Downside of Immutability

Are you comfortable with your data being recorded unchangeably in perpetuity? Those of us born before 1980 have already breathed a sigh of relief that our teenage years and young adulthood were not spent on social media. The idea that our youthful mistakes could be not only public but indelible is worrying. We return to the notions of privacy addressed in Chapter 6: while people seeking anonymity or greater freedoms may be comfortable with a blockchain-based social network, it is not right for the majority. Furthermore, legal provisions such as Europe's General Data Protection Regulations and the Right to be Forgotten require data to be carefully collected, securely stored, and deleted on request.

There is also the very real challenge of archiving. As each block is added to its chain, the volume of data storage required to maintain these increasingly huge distributed ledgers will grow. At what point would you, or could you, close off the tail of the chain? We are asked to keep tax records for up to seven years, but an insurance certificate for employer liability has to be held for decades. The details of a long-term capital project from design onward will need to be authenticated throughout its useful life and at decommissioning, but some of our existing infrastructure is already hundreds of years old. In the fresh dawn of this new technology, there is a rush to put everything on the blockchain: consider the future and choose your immutable records wisely.

Creeping Centralization

The founding principle of cryptocurrency is decentralization: a perfect system of peer-to-peer transactions and randomized validation. Bitcoin still adheres to this vision and Ethereum became rapidly decentralized after the founding team loosened the reins, but other leading cryptocurrencies are arguably much less traditional and more centralized. Specialized blockchains such as EOS with its 21 validating nodes, or Ripple XRP with most tokens still held centrally, are models that skate along the edge of centralization. The rise of what has been dubbed "corpocurrency," starting with the release of the Libra whitepaper, is another source of concern. According to the paper,[7] "An important objective of the Libra Association is to move toward increasing decentralization over time." It suggests that this transition will begin "within five years" from launch, but there is no clear mechanism for the decentralization process.

In blockchain, too, enterprises have tended to opt for permissioned and private blockchains, keeping their commercial cards close to their chests. The frameworks of the Hyperledger project, IBM blockchain, R3 Corda, and specialized Ripple and Stellar systems within the financial back office are designed to work for a known group of participants. The likelihood is that these systems will become more and more open and less centralized as their communities grow, and work is ongoing to identify mechanisms for validation without cryptocurrency, but there is a cloud on the horizon.

As blockchains grow, how do we manage unwieldy trails of blocks going back to genesis 5, 10, 20, or 50 years earlier? Our blockchain structure retains hashed data in perpetuity. Where identity records are concerned, we may still need access to verify information a century on, not to mention the requirements of long lifecycle projects, environmental data, copyright proof, and other applications. Truncating a chain would be an arbitrary process that would almost certainly inconvenience users and could open the whole chain to an attack because it compromises the integrity of the system. A bad actor could conceivably transmit a false version of the history of the chain, and validators would be none the wiser.

If we accept that truncation is not a viable option, then how can we reduce the storage capacity required for all the data that we generate? Estimates suggest that within the next five years, half of the seven billion people on the planet will have at least one record stored on a blockchain. The problem is not going to go away.

One of the solutions that is being proposed is to create a different class of node. At present, all blockchains have nodes that can execute transactions and full nodes that participate in the process of validation and block creation. The suggestion is for the creation of mini-nodes, designed to hold the last few thousand (or more) blocks, and periodically sense-checked against the full chain held by full nodes. The argument is similar to the logic around conventional corporate audit processes: as long as the data structure, the system, and any control functions are working, then the data can be trusted back to the genesis block. This differs from truncation as the whole chain is always available, and the risk of a false history attack is mitigated by regular checks against the original chain. But—and there is always a but—as the chain grows, and the number of nodes able to host the full record falls, there is a danger that the data becomes centralized in the hands of just a few participating full nodes upon which the mini-nodes and transacting nodes rely fully.

The continued expansion of blockchain records and the rise of centrally operated digital cash will impact on the crypto-anarchist ideal of decentralization. It is not, however, an obvious threat in public perception, unlike the latest buzzword on the block: Quantum.

Quantum, Baby!

Will quantum computing wreck the cryptography that underpins blockchain? At almost every forum where people are learning about this technology the question is posed in one form or another. The short answer is that quantum computing is more likely to strengthen encryption than to break it, and as innovator, entrepreneur, 2018 Eisenhower Fellow and former Managing Director of Goldman Sachs William Hurley, known to all as Whurley, says: be inspired, not afraid.

This is not to say that the journey ahead will be plain sailing. While the structure and immutability of a blockchain secured by Proof of Work is very unlikely to be compromised, there are concerns over the security of the data which is held in a hashed form on-chain. Quantum computers in their current state are programmed by physicists, exist in a supercooled

+0.5 Kelvin environment, and perform specific and extraordinarily complex functions that require Qubits of processing power, not bits. The 256-bit encryption that forms the backbone of all current mainstream cryptography, including that which underpins blockchain and cryptocurrency, would be a plaything for a quantum computer to crack.

It is extremely unlikely that quantum computing will be let loose on breaking encryption in the manner of a battle tank against spears. Quantum computing will enable stronger encryption, and blockchain, cryptocurrency, and all other users of cryptography will adopt it. A simple parallel is to look at how our use of passwords has changed over time. It's easy to crack a 1990s password. They were short words, perhaps a number, probably based on the name of your first pet. We now understand that long strings of unrelated words are the most secure option, and we have moved with the times.

Continuing this analogy demonstrates the area of greatest concern around the effect of quantum computing. The structure of a blockchain is secure as long as the encryption used keeps up with the evolution of computing power. Research into the potential impact of quantum computing recognizes that some of the ASIC (algorithm-specific) mining processors in use today come very close to the speed of existing quantum computers. A 2017 paper from Aggarwal et al.[8] concludes that quantum computers would gain no advantage even as they develop. The strength of a consensus mechanism like Proof of Work is that it would take more computing power than is available to change an earlier block and recalculate the algorithm for each subsequent block faster than new blocks are added. Gradual increases in hash power will not affect the integrity of the chain. The real danger is that first, the data that was encrypted in earlier blocks could be deciphered, and second, that quantum processing may be able to compromise the encryption around signatures, deciphering a private key quickly enough to amend or thwart an ongoing transaction.

Developers and enterprises must plan for securing legacy data and minimizing the amount of information that is held on-chain, but this is in line with activity that should already be ongoing for management of archiving and efficient use of a blockchain. There are several initiatives working on more robust blockchain frameworks such as the Quantum Resistant Ledger (QRL) open source community. Technology developed through this route addresses more secure signature systems designed to stand up to future quantum capabilities. Ultimately quantum computing will not break blockchain, but it will cause it to evolve and improve.

Tantalizing Opportunities

There are several potential applications of blockchain that seem at first sight to be straightforward, a good fit for the technology, but which either have hidden complexities or are ideas whose time is yet to come. The financial sector is particularly rich in unrealized potential around improvements to the audit function and the cumbersome system of payment down a multinational supply chain.

Audit and Accountancy

Accounting at its very heart is the recording of transactions with double entry verification, so blockchain is a very relevant technology. It mirrors the audit trail structure of accounting records, making it familiar territory for anyone in the profession, and the immutability and transparency of the records held in a distributed ledger are an attractive proposition. Here is a technology which, if properly implemented, has the potential to improve the authenticity and reliability of records and throw up a barrier to fraud. In the wider context of business, blockchain could also be used as a tool for shareholder management.

Although Northern Trust have been working successfully with auditors PwC and KPMG in respect of private equity transactions, the wider audit landscape is a much more complex arena. New York-based Auditchain have been exploring the role of blockchain in preventing accounting scandals, which hit the headlines on an all too regular basis. The 2001 bankruptcy of the Enron corporation and the subsequent collapse of its "Big Five" auditor, Arthur Andersen, led to the sweeping regulations of the Sarbanes–Oxley Act, yet the problems continued. The year 2018 alone saw the investigation of General Electric (GE) and its de-listing from the Dow Jones index after 122 years, the collapse of several high-profile firms in the United Kingdom including construction giant Carillion, café chain Patisserie Valerie, and retail chain BHS, and the dissolution of the Gupta business empire in South Africa. Auditors came in for severe criticism. KPMG, auditors of GE for over a century, had done nothing to curb what the Securities and Exchange Commission (SEC) described as GE's "aggressive accounting" practices. In the UK they also came under fire from the Financial Reporting Council (FRC) for "rubber-stamping" figures which did not represent the real position of Carillion's business and for a conflict of interest in their lucrative consulting work for the client. They also faced criticism in South Africa where an ex-KPMG auditor from the Gupta team was charged with inappropriate conduct and tax evasion. The FRC reprimanded and fined PwC and individual staff members over the BHS collapse, and criticized Grant Thornton for signing off Patisserie Valerie's accounts without discovering a glaring and fatal hole in its cash balances.

Auditchain is trying to make headway in an industry where regulation is becoming ever tighter but may not be the right solution to the problem. Founder Jason Meyers outlined the core belief that underpins the Auditchain methodology, that system and control objective compliance is the most important part of an audit. If systems are functioning correctly, then the data structure is proper and can be relied upon back to the opening balance. If we put this in the context of a blockchain, then if the most recent few hundred blocks are sampled and found to be correct, the data can be trusted all the way back to the first (genesis) block because the system is functioning correctly. With this degree of compliance, the cost of fraud should become prohibitive.

Accountants and auditors are wary of blockchain because of the prime entry challenge, which we examined in Chapter 4. Blockchain is a cryptographically verifiable record of transactional truths, not a record of absolute truth. Auditors are wary of trusting a ledger without oversight of the source material, which is why my CPA colleagues spent their training years climbing gantries to check that storage tanks were full, and I as a management accountant in manufacturing counted thousands of bolts and screws by hand to verify stock levels. Audit confidence measures are complex, and as Meyers says, blockchain doesn't fit them yet. He also believes there is a perceived threat to the profession from standardization of the audit approach. Wariness preserves both jobs and the consulting revenues, which are based on interpreting ever more onerous regulation.

However, given the recent criticism of the Big Four audit firms in light of high-profile business scandals, there may well be changes coming from within. It is likely that regulators will seek to break the stranglehold of the market leaders and to reinstate the division between consultancy and audit firms which existed until the early 1980s, when Price Waterhouse (later PwC) bought management consultants Urwick Orr and Partners.

When this change comes, Meyers and his colleagues will be ready. Auditchain is the founding member of the DCARPE Alliance, a growing network of early adopters collaborating to prove that there is a better way to perform assurance on an enterprise that enables real-time financial reporting. The Decentralized Continuous Audit and Reporting Protocol Ecosystem divides the systems, control, and data elements of an audit between smaller firms, resulting in an appropriately decentralized cohort of auditors rather than a single firm. The blockchain reports attestations from the auditors under the International Financial Reporting Standards which govern accounting practice. The earliest clients for this approach are businesses already working in the blockchain and cryptocurrency space who are receptive to new ideas and need a solid financial context for their business. This is going to be a fascinating sector to watch and represents a real opportunity for blockchain to offer an appropriate solution to an ever-growing problem.

Commercial Letters of Credit

Although blockchain has claimed its place in cross-border settlements in banking, and in the management of private equity as pioneered by Northern Trust, other financial services could benefit from immutable records, distributed verification, and smart contracts. One example is the existing system of Letters of Credit that reduces commercial risk in import and export.

Paying for goods from people with whom you have no trust relationship is straightforward face-to-face but becomes more complex as soon as the transaction is no longer instantaneous. For this, we rely on establishing trust with intermediaries. At a consumer level, eBay is a good example of a centralized system which helps people to manage the risk associated with making payment and then waiting for goods. It gives buyers confidence to send their money to an unknown seller and has mechanisms in place for a refund in case of problems. It holds sellers to account by making the opinion of buyers transparent through a review system and imposing sanctions in case of default, and protects them as far as possible through prompts to secure payment before delivering goods.

Commercial Letters of Credit, also known as Documentary Credits, are guarantees issued by banks to reassure the seller that funds are available before shipping and that payment will be made as soon as the goods are received. However, at commercial scale, this system is complex and costly. The value of cross-border shipments and the length of time for a cargo to cross the world are many times that of a typical consumer purchase. The commitment by the supplier, particularly when manufacturing or growing goods to order, is significant. The buyer, too, may have to put cash on deposit for the bank to issue its guarantee, tying up working capital for weeks or months.

This is a process that is ripe for disruption if a reliable solution can be implemented at scale. HSBC piloted blockchain-based Letters of Credit on the Voltron platform during 2019, including a yuan-denominated transaction which took 24 hours to complete against the standard ten days[9]. This was a major step toward a commercial model for banks, with lower costs and faster processing, and an important part of the wider push toward a distributed, holistic international supply chain.

Changing societies

Blockchain and other emerging technologies are rapidly changing the way our society operates. There are exciting changes ahead for the majority but concerns that a significant minority are not keeping up. Even in countries with universal access to learning there is a remarkably high proportion of the population who are not digitally literate. In the United States, it was reported in 2019 that 10 percent of Americans did not go online, and in the United Kingdom a similar study identified that almost a fifth of Britons did not use the internet.[10] In both countries this included older citizens and also, significantly, demographics with lower educational attainment and household income. We have already seen how unbanked citizens in a banked economy are disadvantaged, but if this group cannot access the decentralized online communities which characterize our brave new world they will be left behind. A changing society must include education and support to harness opportunities.

Rewarding the Creator

One of the most prized goals for blockchain is the democratization of earnings. This goes right back to the Crypto Anarchist Manifesto,[11] which envisioned "a liquid market for any and all material which can be put into words and pictures." Blockchain offers a mechanism for financial inclusion for producers and creators, and the work already ongoing in the provenance of goods and the traceability of commodities through the supply chain makes the source of such items transparent. In Chapter 5 we also looked at the role of blockchain, particularly nonfungible tokens, in the music industry and supply chain, and the ongoing work which is gaining traction in managing a complex, borderless royalties system.

Ensuring that there are appropriate rewards for producers of the physical is something that has already been championed by the Fair-Trade Foundation and similar organizations throughout the world long before the advent of blockchain. The role of blockchain here is not to disrupt but to offer a tool to help the established systems. Blockchain may help to reduce the cost of credit to producers and manage the "last mile" of cash. Ensuring that payment reaches the right people, and that any losses in cross-border settlement are minimized, may be a role for cryptocurrency. Fair Trade also recognize the potential of blockchain in the decentralization and democratization of information.[12] Their hope is that it "could support farmers to understand the journeys their crops take—potentially helping them to better manage their customer relationships and risks—and ultimately become more resilient."

So, what of digital assets? These lend themselves immediately to management through a distributed ledger, using the same mechanism as provenance applications examined in Chapter 4. The difference here is that authenticating ownership is not enough on its own. Provenance records move forward as goods change hands, and to reward the creator money must flow backward to source. The management of owned assets seems an obvious use case for a ledger, and as we saw in Chapter 6 registries are gradually moving toward distributed systems for everything from parcels of land to life records. The pattern of ownership of any asset can be complex, and subdivision and shared ownership are common. These are not only a matter of record but also lend themselves to tokenization.

Representing financial instruments and both virtual and physical investment assets as tokens opens up possibilities for new commercial activities. While managing the provenance and traceability of tangible assets such as diamonds, artwork, and luxury goods is commercially established, extending the principle to shares and securities or even investment properties is in the very early stages of realization. Exploring this type of tokenization indicates potential to increase liquidity for trading and offers opportunities for crowdfunding and equity release. Representing assets with tokens could move us toward peer-to-peer nonmonetary asset exchange.

Data and Identity

When did you last buy a service using your data as currency? Was it the airport wi-fi, or the one in the hotel, coffee shop, or train? I'm sure you read all the terms and conditions as you entered your name and e-mail address and exposed your data to an unknown network. Or perhaps it was the latest game on Facebook. Concerns are regularly raised around the data retained by viral apps and by Facebook themselves[13] who require "a non-exclusive, transferable, sub-licensable, royalty-free, and worldwide license to host, use, distribute, modify, run, copy, publicly perform or display, translate, and create derivative works of your content." The big tech giants see the continuum from privacy to personalization as a consumer choice. Speaking at SXSW in 2016, Microsoft's Mike Hintze and Google's Keith Enright talked of empowering users, engineering for trust, and managing the sensitivities of individuals to start to personalize the privacy experience. Ethics in the digital world are under the spotlight. Google and Apple, among others, have reportedly hired in-house philosophers.[14] The Center for Digital Ethics and Policy at Loyola University Chicago develops best practice and guidelines regarding ethical behavior in online and digital environments, hosts an annual International Symposium on Digital Ethics, and publishes essays on the ethics of everything from artificial intelligence and ownership of personal data[15] to self-driving cars.

If we do not give up some personal data, how are we to be identified? Proving personal identity effectively has been a challenge for generations. Partial solutions for the physical confirmation of identity are applied piecemeal across the world. Crossing national borders generally requires an identity card or passport, some but not all of which may detail the holder's home address alongside their name, nationality, and birth details. Screening could also involve providing (in the author's recent personal experience) some, all, or none of: thumb prints, index fingerprints, full sets of prints, retinal scans, facial recognition scans, and full contact details and travel plans while in the country. Within individual countries, identity cards may be either ubiquitous or absent, and the recording of births might be immediate and precise, or informal to the point that official documents routinely record birth dates as January 1, in the absence of any detail other than the year of birth.

Digitally, there are multiple pseudo-identity systems allowing us to move seamlessly between software produced by individual providers, and often used to verify our identity with third party software. In 2016, Apple confirmed they had one billion active devices, all attached to an Apple ID. Facebook's two billion users can "log in with Facebook" to multiple applications. Microsoft accounts control access to the whole suite of tools produced by the company. The landscape is messy and the accounts themselves are effectively anonymous, because users self-certify as real humans. Fake accounts proliferate. The technology to link accounts with services is good, but in situations where verification of account holder identity is genuinely required, for example in accessing taxation services or banking software, the process reverts to physical proofs.

It's a confusing picture, and one where control is centralized, and reams of personal data are vulnerable to hacking and theft. Blockchain technology has the potential to deliver a single proof of identity with distributed verification. An individual's identity blockchain could begin with the registration of their birth, and incorporate life events such as vaccinations, qualifications, voter registration, and location changes as they occur. The records are immutable, data sources distributed, and there is no centralized control. In terms of security, although individual blocks may be accessed, the whole chain of information would not be visible. Currently, if an ID document is presented for proof of age it may also reveal place of birth and current address. Under principles of data protection and privacy, being able to reveal only the birth date block in a reliable record is preferable. Although there are significant innovations around digital identity from Estonia to ID2020 to the World Food Programme, achieving a joined up, global system of both identity records and acceptance is many years away.

Save the Tooth Fairy

Possibly the most difficult question I asked of the many people who generously gave their time to assist in researching this book was: what will the Tooth Fairy put under the pillow if we move to a cashless world?

DLA Piper's Martin Bartlam speculated that even now, children do not appreciate the value of money until long after the Tooth Fairy has stopped visiting. They see their parents ordering goods online and using contactless cards to make payments in store; cash is a rarity. Is the Tooth Fairy tradition one that will fade with us, the last generation to appreciate cash? Our attachment to the medium is increasingly sentimental. "How else will you play shove ha'penny or decide important yes/no questions in your life?" asked author Mark Hayes. "Tossing a barcode is never going to work." The ubiquitous smart devices that already hold our children's attention may be the answer, said FinTech speaker Liz Lumley. Will the Tooth Fairy send a text message, "Your account has been updated," or a cartoon tale of tooth collection and appropriate remuneration for younger readers? Anne Ahola Ward of Veritoken suggested a simple and oddly comforting message: "Your tooth is in the cloud." Whatever happens, our world is going to change in ways we cannot imagine.

References

Hyperlinks and documents accessed January 2020

Chapter 1

1. Stoll, C. February 1995. "Why the Web Won't be Nirvana." *Newsweek* https://newsweek.com/clifford-stoll-why-web-wont-be-nirvana-185306

2. Hyponnen, M. April 2019. @Mikko *Twitter* https://twitter.com/mikko/status/1120311404660236288

3. Brin, D. "Earth: A Prediction Engine?" [Website] http://davidbrin.com/earth.html

4. Cellan-Jones, R. October 2018 "Could Blockchain solve Irish Border Issue?" *BBC News* https://bbc.co.uk/news/technology-45725572

5. Roubini, N., Prof. October 2018 "*Testimony for the Hearing of the U.S. Senate Committee on Banking, Housing and Community Affairs on "Exploring the Cryptocurrency and Blockchain Ecosystem*" https://banking.senate.gov/imo/media/doc/Roubini%20Testimony%2010-11-18.pdf

6. UN Blockchain, Multi-UN Agency Platform [Website] https://un-blockchain.org/

7. Hrones, M. July 2018. "Yes, Your Bitcoin Transactions Can Be Tracked—And Here Are The Companies That Are Doing It." *The Bitcoinist* https://bitcoinist.com/yes-your-bitcoin-transactions-can-be-tracked-and-here-are-the-companies-that-are-doing-it/

8. May 2017. "Marcus Hutchins 'Saved the U.S.' From WannaCry Cyberattack on Bedroom Computer", *NBC News* https://nbcnews.com/storyline/hacking-of-america/marcus-hutchins-saved-u-s-wannacry-cyberattack-bedroom-compter-n759931

9. April-August 2017 Blockchain Explorer, WannaCry ransom wallet transactions, https://blockchain.com/btc/address/12t9YDPgwuez9NyMgw519p7AA8isjr6SMw

10. PonziCoin [Website] https://ponzicoin.co/home.html

11. Harari, Y.N. 2014 "Sapiens: A Brief History of Humankind." *Harvill Secker.* ISBN 978-1846558238. Excerpt from Chapter 10 https://ynharari.com/topic/money-and-politics/

12. February 2019 California Legislature Assembly Bill No. 953 https://leginfo.legislature.ca.gov/faces/billTextClient.xhtml?bill_id=201920200AB953

13. Long, C. June 2019. "What Facebook's Cryptocurrency Means: 6 Predictions." *Forbes* https://forbes.com/sites/caitlinlong/2019/06/09/what-facebooks-cryptocurrency-means-6-predictions/#6a9b131e7022

14. May 2019. Bitcoin Block Explorer, Block Height 575171 (searchable) https://blockexplorer.com/
15. July 2018. "Blockchain Based Evidence Approved in China." *Dr Meyer-Dulheuer & Partners LLP* https://legal-patent.com/international-intellectual-property/blockchain-based-evidence-approved-china/
16. Merkle, R.J. 1979. "Secrecy, Authentication, and Public Key Systems." [Thesis] https://merkle.com/papers/Thesis1979.pdf

Chapter 2

1. Chaum, D. 1982. "Computer Systems Established, Maintained and Trusted by Mutually Suspicious Groups [Dissertation]." UC Berkeley. https://chaum.com/publications/research_chaum_2.pdf
2. Chaum, D. 1982. *Blind Signatures for Untraceable Payments.* https://chaum.com/publications/Chaum-blind-signatures.PDF
3. Levy, S. January 1994. "E-Money (That's What I Want)." *Wired Business.* https://wired.com/1994/12/emoney/
4. May, T.C. 1988. "The Crypto Anarchist Manifesto." https://activism.net/cypherpunk/crypto-anarchy.html
5. Levy, S. December 2001. "Crypto: How the Code Rebels Beat the Government Saving Privacy in the Digital Age." Penguin Books. https://amazon.com/Crypto-Rebels-Government-Privacy-Digital/dp/0140244328
6. May, T.C. 1988. "The Crypto Anarchist Manifesto." https://activism.net/cypherpunk/crypto-anarchy.html
7. Assange, J. November 2012. *Cypherpunks: Freedom and the Future of the Internet.* OR Books, ISBN 978-1-939293-00-8 https://orbooks.com/catalog/cypherpunks/
8. Wei Dai, 1988. *B-money.* http://weidai.com/bmoney.txt
9. Kingsley. P. August 2012. "The Financial Crisis Timeline." *The Guardian.* https://theguardian.com/business/2012/aug/07/credit-crunch-boom-bust-timeline
10. Nakamoto, S. October 2008. "Bitcoin: A Peer-to-Peer Electronic Cash System." https://bitcoin.org/bitcoin.pdf
11. Szabo, N. December 2005. "Bit Gold." https://nakamotoinstitute.org/bit-gold/
12. Alvarez, J. March 2019. "Who is Satoshi Nakamoto? We Look at the Possible Candidates." *Blockonomi.* https://blockonomi.com/who-is-satoshi-nakamoto/
13. Redman, J. January 2017. "Bitcoin's Quirky Genesis Block Turns Eight Years Old Today." *Bitcoin.com News.* https://news.bitcoin.com/bitcoins-quirky-genesis-block-turns-eight-years-old-today/

14. U.S. Copyright Office. May 22, 2019. "Press Release: Questions about Certain Bitcoin Registrations."https://copyright.gov/press-media-info/press-updates.html

15. Kelly, J. August 2019. "He's not Satoshi, He's a Very Naughty Boy." *Financial Times* https://ftalphaville.ft.com/2019/08/27/1566922213000/He-s-not-Satoshi-he-s-a-very-naughty-boy/

16. Willett, J.R. 2013. "San Jose Bitcoin Conference." YouTube (from 4:19) https://youtu.be/4bMf4xZg_4U?t=4m19s

17. Shin, L. September 2017. "Here's The Man Who Created ICOs And This Is The New Token He's Backing." *Forbes.* https://forbes.com/sites/laurashin/2017/09/21/heres-the-man-who-created-icos-and-this-is-the-new-token-hes-backing/#6d5ffea31183

18. Buterin, V. Ethereum Whitepaper [live version] https://github.com/ethereum/wiki/wiki/White-Paper

19. Buterin, V. December 2013. "Ethereum: A Next Generation Smart Contract and Decentralized Application Platform." [Original whitepaper] http://blockchainlab.com/pdf/Ethereum_white_paper-a_next_generation_smart_contract_and_decentralized_application_platform-vitalik-buterin.pdf

20. Dhameja, G. February 2019. "UN World Food Programme Uses Parity Ethereum to Aid 100,000 Refugees." *Parity Technologies* https://parity.io/un-world-food-programme-uses-parity-ethereum-to-aid-100-000-refugees/

21. Back, A. August 2002. "Hashcash—A Denial of Service Counter-Measure." http://hashcash.org/papers/hashcash.pdf

22. Lamport, L, R. Shostak, and M. Pease. 1982. "The Byzantine Generals Problem." *SRI International.* https://people.eecs.berkeley.edu/~luca/cs174/byzantine.pdf

23. Proof of Work cryptocurrencies. *Cryptoslate.* https://cryptoslate.com/cryptos/proof-of-work/

24. Ongaro, D., and J. Ousterhout. 2014. "In Search of an Understandable Consensus Algorithm" *Stanford University* https://usenix.org/system/files/conference/atc14/atc14-paper-ongaro.pdf

Chapter 3

1. NXT [website] https://nxtplatform.org/
2. Augur [website] https://augur.net/
3. Wolfson, R., A. Killeen, G. Beyda, and J. Song. 2019. "Why VCs have Joined the Block Party" *SXSW Panel* https://schedule.sxsw.com/2019/events/PP87883
4. Alexandre, A. July 2018. "New Study Says 80 Percent of ICOs Conducted in 2017 Were Scams." *CoinTelegraph* https://cointelegraph.com/news/new-study-says-80-percent-of-icos-conducted-in-2017-were-scams

5. Lyons, D. 2018. "Lab Rats: How Silicon Valley Made Work Miserable for the Rest of Us." *Hachette Books* https://amazon.com/Lab-Rats-Silicon-Valley-Miserable/dp/031656186X

6. Robinson, M., and M. Leising. June 2018. "Tether Used to Manipulate Price of Bitcoin During 2017 Peak: New Study." *Bloomberg* https://bloomberg.com/news/articles/2018-06-13/professor-who-rang-vix-alarm-says-tether-used-to-boost-bitcoin

7. February 2019. "Warren Buffett says bitcoin is a 'delusion' and 'attracts charlatans." *CNBC* https://cnbc.com/2019/02/25/warren-buffett-says-bitcoin-is-a-delusion.html

8. Roubini, N. Prof. *Testimony for the Hearing of the U.S. Senate Committee on Banking, Housing and Community Affairs on "Exploring the Cryptocurrency and Blockchain Ecosystem"* https://banking.senate.gov/imo/media/doc/Roubini%20Testimony%2010-11-18.pdf

9. Remarks at the Yahoo Finance All Markets Summit: Crypto, William Hinman, SEC, June 2018 https://sec.gov/news/speech/speech-hinman-061418

10. Hinman, W., and V. Szczepanik. April 2019. "Statement on 'Framework for 'Investment Contract' Analysis of Digital Assets." U.S. Securities and Exchange Commission, https://sec.gov/news/public-statement/statement-framework-investment-contract-analysis-digital-assets

11. Klayman, J.A. April 2019. "Don't Call It A Comeback: With Two Bills, U.S. Lawmakers Aim To Give New Life to Non-Security Tokens." *Forbes* https://forbes.com/sites/joshuaklayman/2019/04/13/dont-call-it-a-comeback-with-new-bills-u-s-lawmakers-aim-to-give-new-life-to-non-security-tokens/#53d8d0b5900f

12. Financial Conduct Authority. 2019. *Guidance on Cryptoassets*, https://fca.org.uk/publications/consultation-papers/cp19-3-guidance-cryptoassets

13. Inman, P. August 2019 "Mark Carney: dollar is too dominant and could be replaced by digital currency." *The Guardian* https://theguardian.com/business/2019/aug/23/mark-carney-dollar-dominant-replaced-digital-currency

14. PACTE law (Original commentary in French). April 2019. https://economie.gouv.fr/loi-pacte-encourager-innovation-france

15. Total Cryptos. *Cryptoslate* https://cryptoslate.com/coins/

16. Buchholz, K. June 2019. "How Common is Crypto." *Statista* https://statista.com/chart/18345/crypto-currency-adoption/

17. Albornoz, C. June 2019. (Original post in Spanish). *Twitter* https://twitter.com/CarlosOAlbornoz/status/1141122355172958208

18. DiSalvo, M. December 2018. "Why Colombia has Become a Hotspot for Bitcoin ATMs" *news.Bitcoin.com* https://news.bitcoin.com/why-colombia-has-become-a-hotspot-for-bitcoin-atms/

19. 2017 FDIC National Survey of Unbanked and Underbanked Households https://fdic.gov/householdsurvey/
20. Antonopoulos, A.M. June 19, 2019. "Libra Not Libra: Facebook's Blockchain Project" *Talk at the Scottish Blockchain Meetup.* https://www.youtube.com/watch?v=7S6506vkth4&vl=en
21. Palmer, D. November 2018. "Victims Sue AT&T, T-Mobile Over 'SIM Swap' Crypto Hacks." *Coindesk,* https://coindesk.com/victims-sue-att-t-mobile-over-sim-swap-crypto-hacks
22. Ngo, D. March 2015. "QuadrigaCX to Become World's First Publicly Traded Bitcoin Exchange." *CoinTelegraph* https://cointelegraph.com/news/quadrigacx-to-become-worlds-first-publicly-traded-bitcoin-exchange
23. June 2019. Ernst and Young, Supreme Court of Nova Scotia Hfx No. 484742. Fifth report of the Monitor in Quadriga Fintech Solutions Corp [CCAA Monitor and Trustee in Bankruptcy] P6 https://documentcentre.eycan.com/eycm_library/Quadriga%20Fintech%20Solutions%20Corp/English/CCAA/1.%20Monitor's%20Reports/6.%20Fifth%20Report%20of%20the%20Monitor/Fifth%20Report%20of%20the%20Monitor%20dated%20June%2019,%202019.PDF
24. Long, C. June 2019. "Bitcoin, The Dollar And Facebook's Cryptocurrency: Price Volatility Versus Systemic Volatility." *Forbes,* https://forbes.com/sites/caitlinlong/2019/06/29/bitcoin-the-dollar-and-facebooks-cryptocurrency-price-volatility-versus-systemic-volatility/#2432ff0788b8

Chapter 4

1. Cellan-Jones, R. October 2018. "Could Blockchain Solve Irish Border Issue?" *BBC News* https://bbc.co.uk/news/technology-45725572
2. Eden, T. June 2018. "How I Became Leonardo da Vinci on the Blockchain." https://shkspr.mobi/blog/2018/06/how-i-became-leonardo-da-vinci-on-the-blockchain/
3. Huckle, S., R. Bhattacharya, M. White, and N. Beloff. 2016. "Internet of Things, Blockchain and Shared Economy Applications." *Procedia Computer Science* 98, pp. 461–466. ISSN 1877-0509 https://doi.org/10.1016/j.procs.2016.09.074
4. Bell, M., A. Green, J. Sheridan, J. Collomosse, D. Cooper, T. Bui, O. Thereaux and J. Higgins. 2019 "Underscoring Archival Authenticity with Blockchain Technology," *Insights* 32, no. 21, pp. 1–7; DOI: https://doi.org/10.1629/uksg.470
5. Dickson, B. June 2019. "Can Anything Protect Us from Deepfakes?" *PCMag* https://uk.pcmag.com/opinion/121370/can-anything-protect-us-from-deepfakes

6. The Diamond Time-Lapse Protocol https://www.everledger.io/pdfs/Press-Release-Everledger-Announces-the-Industry-Diamond-Time-Lapse-Protocol.pdf

7. Skinner, C. January 2019. "The heart of the Blockchain Use Case: Digital Proof (Everledger case study)" https://thefinanser.com/2016/01/the-heart-of-the-blockchain-use-case-digital-proof.html/

8. May 2019. "LVMH, ConsenSys and Microsoft Announce AURA, a Consortium to Power the Luxury Industry with Blockchain Technology." https://content.consensys.net/wp-content/uploads/AURA_ConsenSys_Press-Release_May-16-2019-2.pdf

9. IBM Food Trust [website] https://ibm.com/blockchain/solutions/food-trust

10. McKenzie, J. February 2018. "Why Blockchain won't Fix Food Safety—Yet" *The New Food Economy* https://newfoodeconomy.org/blockchain-food-traceability-walmart-ibm/

11. Cosgrove, E. April 2019. "IBM's Blockchain for Food Gains Major U.S. Grocer." *Supply Chain Dive* https://supplychaindive.com/news/ibm-blockchain-for-food-gains-major-us-grocer/552647/

12. Zmudzinski, A. June 2019. "National Fisheries Institute and IBM's Food Trust Work on Seafood Blockchain Traceability." *Cointelegraph* https://cointelegraph.com/news/national-fisheries-institute-and-ibms-food-trust-work-on-seafood-blockchain-traceability

13. July 2019. "Millions of Durians will be Tracked on the Blockchain for Thailand's Largest Exporter." *Fintech News* http://fintechnews.sg/32244/thailand/durian-blockchain-tracking/

14. Clauson, K.A., E.A. Breeden, C. Davidson, and T.K. Mackey. March 2018 "Leveraging Blockchain Technology to Enhance Supply Chain Management in Healthcare: An Exploration of Challenges and Opportunities in the Health Supply Chain." *Blockchain in Healthcare Today* SSN 2573-8240 https://doi.org/10.30953/bhty.v1.20

15. Wolfson, R. June 2019. "Merck and Walmart Will Track Prescription Drugs On IBM Blockchain In FDA Pilot." *Forbes,* https://forbes.com/sites/rachelwolfson/2019/06/13/merck-and-walmart-will-track-prescription-drugs-on-ibm-blockchain-in-fda-pilot/#76ab6a94212e

16. Microsoft. May 2018. "Ground-Breaking Insurance Blockchain Solution Runs on Microsoft Azure." https://customers.microsoft.com/en-us/story/insurwave-insurance-azure/

17. Garnsey, S. September 2018. "Kuehne + Nagel builds in blockchain." *Automotive Logistics* https://automotivelogistics.media/news/kuehne-nagel-builds-blockchain

18. "VisiCalc of Dan Bricklin and Bob Frankston" *History of the Computer* https://history-computer.com/ModernComputer/Software/Visicalc.html

19. Browne, R. April. 2018. "Santander Launches a Blockchain-Based Foreign Exchange Service that uses Ripple's Technology" *CNBC* https://cnbc.com/2018/04/12/santander-launches-blockchain-based-foreign-exchange-using-ripple-tech.html

20. March 2018. Credit Suisse and ING execute First Live Transaction using HQLAx Securities Lending app on R3's Corda Blockchain Platform. https://credit-suisse.com/corporate/en/articles/media-releases/cs-and-ing-execute-first-live-transaction-201803.html

21. March 2018. "Northern Trust strengthens Private Equity Audit Via Blockchain Technology with PwC." https://www.businesswire.com/news/home/20180319005240/en/Northern-Trust-Strengthens-Private-Equity-Audit-Blockchain

22. June 2019. "Northern Trust to Transfer Pioneering Private Equity Blockchain Technology Platform to Broadridge." https://northerntrust.com/united-kingdom/pr/2019/northern-trust-to-transfer-pe-blockchain-technology-to-broadridge

23. Official website for the States of Guernsey, Income Tax (Substance Requirements) (Implementation) (Amendment) Regulations, 2018, https://gov.gg/economicsubstance

24. April 2019. "Northern Trust Marks a Breakthrough in Securities Servicing by Deploying Legal Clauses as Smart Contracts on Blockchain." *Northern Trust* https://northerntrust.com/united-kingdom/pr/2019/northern-trust-securities-services-deploys-blockchain-smart-contracts

25. Azaria, A., A. Ekblaw, T. Vieira, and A. Lippman. 2016. "MedRec: Using Blockchain for Medical Data Access and Permission Management." *IEEE* https://doi.org/10.1109/OBD.2016.11

26. Skelton, S.K. April 2019. "Payroll software provider pilots use of blockchain in human resources" *Computer Weekly* https://computerweekly.com/news/252461189/Payroll-software-provider-pilots-use-of-blockchain-in-human-resources

27. Siemens Digital Grid [Website] https://new.siemens.com/global/en/company/topic-areas/microgrids.html

28. Burger, C., A. Kuhlmann, P. Richard, and J. Weinmann. November 2016. "Blockchain in the Energy Transition: A Survey Among Decision-Makers in the German Energy Industry." *DENA* https://www.esmt.org/system/files_force/dena_esmt_studie_blockchain_english.pdf?download=1

29. Andoni, M., V. Robu, D. Flynn, S. Abram, D. Geach, D. Jenkins, P. McCallum, and A. Peacock. 2019. "Blockchain Technology in the Energy Sector: A systematic Review of Challenges and Opportunities." *Renewable and Sustainable Energy Reviews* 100, pp. 143–174 https://doi.org/10.1016/j.rser.2018.10.014

30. Engie [Website] https://engie.com/en/businesses/microgrids-decentralized-energy/

31. Benton, D., B. Cullen, G. Dennis, L. Dignard-Bailey, T. El-Fouly, C. Ianniciello, A. Pape-Salmon, S. Wong, and M. Wrinch. September 2013. "The First Canadian Smart Remote Microgrid: Hartley Bay BC." *International Microgrid Symposium, Santiago, Chile* https://researchgate.net/publication/311734710_The_First_Canadian_Smart_Remote_Microgrid_Hartley_Bay_British_Columbia

32. LO3 Energy [Website] https://lo3energy.com/innovations/

33. June 2006. "ABLE UK Forges Ahead with Plans to Scrap U.S. 'Ghost Ships.'" *The Maritime Executive.* https://maritime-executive.com/article/2006-06-01able-uk-forges-ahead-with-plans-to-scr

34. Hackitt, J. May 2018. "Building a Safer Future—Independent Review of Building Regulations and Fire Safety: Final Report." https://assets.publishing.service.gov.uk/government/uploads/system/uploads/attachment_data/file/707785/Building_a_Safer_Future_-_web.pdf

Chapter 5

1. March 2019 The Web Foundation @WebFoundation on Twitter https://twitter.com/webfoundation/status/1105544272827371523

2. October 2012. Eugene Jarecki recalls playing Empire on PLATO *Plato History* http://platohistory.org/blog/games/

3. Jenkins, G. September 2018. "Let's fix the player's ownership" *Blockchain Game Summit* https://youtube.com/watch?v=thwJ7PA4Rmw

4. Evans, S. October 2018 "Premier League Launches Esports Competition for Gamers." *Reuters* https://uk.reuters.com/article/uk-soccer-england-esports/premier-league-launches-esports-competition-for-gamers-idUKKCN1ME1PN

5. Noble, J. May 2019. "Norris learned about Verstappen's style in simracing." *Motorsports* https://motorsport.com/f1/news/norris-verstappen-learned-simracing-games/4398421/

6. Muzzy, E. January 2018 "Cryptokitties Isn't About the Cats." *Medium* https://medium.com/@everett.muzzy/cryptokitties-isnt-about-the-cats-aef47bcde92d

7. December 2017. "CryptoKitties Craze Slows Down Transactions on Ethereum." *BBC News* https://bbc.co.uk/news/technology-42237162

8. Radomski, W. June 2019. "ERC-1155: The Final Token Standard on Ethereum." *Medium* https://blog.enjincoin.io/erc-1155-the-final-token-standard-on-ethereum-a83fce9f5714

9. Chong, N. September 2018. "World's Most Expensive Cryptokitty Sells for 600 ETH." *Ethereum World News* https://ethereumworldnews.com/worlds-expensive-cryptokitty-600-eth/

10. Happe, R. 2019 "2019 Edition of the Community Maturity Model." *The Community Roundtable* https://communityroundtable.com/best-practices/2019-edition-of-the-community-maturity-model/

11. January 2019. "Cryptokitties X Gods Unchained." *Fuel Games on Medium* https://medium.com/@fuelgames/cryptokitties-x-gods-unchained-7f69c80b5e5b

12. NFT License [Website] https://niftylicense.org/

13. Velez, J. July 2019. "Imogen Heap on How Musicians can Thrive in a Technology-Driven World." *Grammys* https://www.grammy.com/grammys/news/imogen-heap-how-musicians-can-thrive-technology-driven-world

14. Lyons, F., H. Sun, D.P. Collopy, D, P. O'Hagan, and K. Curran. June 2019. "Music 2025—The Music Data Dilemma: Issues Facing the Music Industry in Improving Data Management." *Intellectual Property Office* https://gov.uk/government/publications/music-2025-the-music-data-dilemma

15. Musicoin [Website] https://musicoin.org

16. Visa Annual report 2018 https://s1.q4cdn.com/050606653/files/doc_financials/annual/2018/Visa-2018-Annual-Report-FINAL.pdf

17. PayPal Annual Report 2018 https://investor.paypal-corp.com/news-releases/news-release-details/paypal-reports-fourth-quarter-and-full-year-2018-results

18. Gilad, Y., R. Hemo, S. Micali, G. Vlachos, and N. Zeldovich. October 2017. "Algorand: Scaling Byzantine Agreements for Cryptocurrencies." https://doi.org/10.1145/3132747.3132757

19. Back, A, M. Corallo, L. Dashjr, M. Friedenback, G. Maxwell, A. Miller, A. Poelstra, J. Timón, and P. Wuille. October 2014. "Enabling Blockchain Innovations with Pegged Sidechains" https://blockstream.com/sidechains.pdf

20. Poon, J., and T. Dryja. January 2016. "The Bitcoin Lightning Network: Scalable Off-Chain Instant Payments" https://lightning.network/lightning-network-paper.pdf

Chapter 6

1. April 2018. Jeremy Fleming, Director GCHQ Speech at CyberUK Conference. https://gchq.gov.uk/speech/director-cyber-uk-speech-2018

2. Brin, D. 1999. "The Transparent Society: Will Technology Force Us To Choose Between Privacy And Freedom?" ISBN 978-0738201443 https://www.amazon.com/Transparent-Society-Technology-Between-Privacy/dp/0738201448

3. Buldas, A., and M. Saarepera. 2004. "On Provably Secure Time-Stamping Schemes." https://link.springer.com/content/pdf/10.1007%2F 978-3-540-30539-2_35.pdf

4. ID2020: An Alliance Committed to Improving Lives through Digital Identity [Website] https://id2020.org/

5. Irrera, A. June 2017. "Accenture, Microsoft Team Up on Blockchain-Based Digital ID Network." *Reuters* https://uk.reuters.com/article/us-microsoft-accenture-digitalid/accenture-microsoft-team-up-on-blockchain-based-digital-id-network-idUKKBN19A22B

6. Shin, L. May 2018. "The UN World Food Programme's Blockchain-Based Food Vouchers for Syrian Refugees, With Robert Opp." *Unconfirmed Podcast* Ep. 017 https://unconfirmed.libsyn.com/the-un-world-food-programmes-blockchain-based-food-vouchers-for-syrian-refugees-with-robert-opp-ep017

7. July 2019. "DIFC, Mashreq Bank, Norbloc Join Hands for Blockchain KYC Consortium." *Khaleej Times* https://khaleejtimes.com/business/corporate/ difc-mashreq-bank-norbloc-join-hands-for-blockchain-kyc-consortium

8. December 2018. "Fourteen French Corporates Complete Regional CordaKYC Trial." *Finextra* https://finextra.com/pressarticle/76605/fourteen-french-corporates-complete-regional-cordakyc-trial/transaction

9. State of Wyoming Legislature 2019 SF0125—Digital Assets-Existing Law https://wyoleg.gov/Legislation/2019/sf0125

10. Benbunan-Fich, R., and A. Castellanos. 2018. "Digitalization of Land Records: From Paper to Blockchain." *Thirty Ninth International Conference on Information Systems, San Francisco 2018 https://www.researchgate.net/ publication/329222337_Digitalization_of_Land_Records_From_Paper_to_ Blockchain*

11. July 2018. "Propy Announces the First California Property Sale on the Blockchain." *BusinessWire* https://businesswire.com/news/home/201807 23005199/en/Propy-Announces-California-Property-Sale-Blockchain

12. October 2018 "Blockchain Used to Sell Real Estate for the First Time in the EU." *PR Newswire* https://prnewswire.com/news-releases/blockchain-used-to-sell-real-estate-for-the-first-time-in-the-eu-808847530.html

13. Smart Dubai blockchain strategy. https://smartdubai.ae/initiatives/ blockchain [website].

14. August 2019, Treasury Board of Canada Secretariat. "Minister Murray Launches New Policy on Service and Digital Strengthening Commitment to Digital Government." https://canada.ca/en/treasury-board-secretariat/ news/2019/08/minister-murray-launches-new-policy-on-service-and-digital-strengthening-commitment-to-digital-government.html

15. Schneider, S. May 2019. "Is Electronic Voting a Political Risk?" *NewStatesman* https://newstatesman.com/spotlight/cyber/2019/05/electronic -voting-political-risk

16. Feng, H., D. Clarke, B. Randell, and S. Shahandashti. 2018. "Verifiable Classroom Voting in Practice." *IEEE Security and Privacy* 16, no. 1, pp. 72–81, *2018.* https://eprint.iacr.org/2017/056.pdf

17. Sallal, M, S. Schneider, M. Casey, C. Dragan, F. Dupressoir, J. Han, L. Riley, H. Treharne, and J. Wadsworth. 2018. "VMV: Augmenting Internet Voting Systems with Selene Verifiability using Permissioned Distributed Ledger." *University of Surrey* https://vmv.surrey.ac.uk/assets/vmv-a70d5586766561ed edb358fc874d11f69f0a53c9ce2a7414129587eb5acba4ad.pdf

18. Pilkington, M. September 2015. "Blockchain Technology: Principles and Applications." *Research Handbook on Digital Transformations,* ed. F. Xavier Olleros and M. Zhegu. Edward Elgar https://ssrn.com/abstract=2662660

19. Kelly, M. November 2018. "Nearly 150 West Virginians Voted with a Mobile Blockchain App." *The Verge* https://theverge.com/2018/11/10/18080518/ blockchain-voting-mobile-app-west-virginia-voatz

20. September 2018. "WVSOS Mobile Voting App Test Pilot Project for November 2018 General Election" *West Virginia Secretary of State, YouTube* https://youtu.be/I8Mphur0YEU

21. Warren, S.D., and L.D. Brandeis. December 1890. "The Right to Privacy." *Harvard Law Review* 4, no. 5, pp. 193–220. Stable URL: http://links.jstor. org/sici?sici=0017-811X%2818901215%294%3A5%3C193%3ATRTP%3 E2.0.CO%3B2-C

Chapter 7

1. Bitcoin Energy Consumption, *Digiconomist* https://digiconomist.net/ bitcoin-energy-consumption

2. Vranken, H. 2017. "Sustainability of Bitcoin and Blockchains." *Current Opinion in Environmental Sustainability* 28, pp. 1–9. https://doi. org/10.1016/j.cosust.2017.04.011

3. Bendiksen, C., and S. Gibbons. June 2019. "The Bitcoin Mining Network— Trends, Composition, Average Creation Cost, Electricity Consumption & Sources." *CoinShares Research.* https://coinsharesgroup.com/assets/resources/ Research/bitcoin-mining-network-june-2019-fidelity-foreword.pdf

4. The Fightback Against the Bitcoin Energy Guzzlers has Begun https://wired. co.uk/article/bitcoin-mining-energy-consumption-new-york

5. De Vries, A. 2019. "Renewable Energy Will Not Solve Bitcoin's Sustainability Problem." *Joule* 3, no. 4, pp. 893–898 https://doi.org/10.1016/j.joule.2019 .02.007

6. 2018 "Blockchain Could Enable $1 Trillion in Trade, Mostly for SMEs and Emerging Markets." *World Economic Forum*, September 2018 https://www. weforum.org/agenda/2018/09/blockchain-set-to-increase-global-trade-by-1- trillion/

7. June 2019. Libra White Paper s 05 The Libra Association https://libra.org/en-US/white-paper

8. Aggarwal, D., G.K. Brennan, T. Lee, M. Santha, and M. Tomamichel. 2017. "Quantum Attacks on Bitcoin, and How to Protect Against Them." https://arxiv.org/pdf/1710.10377.pdf

9. John, A. September 2019. "HSBC Processes First Blockchain Letter of Credit using Chinese yuan." *Reuters.* https://uk.reuters.com/article/us-hsbc-hldg-blockchain/hsbc-processes-first-blockchain-letter-of-credit-using-chinese-yuan-idUSKCN1VN1QL

10. Ward, M. September 2019. "Almost One-Fifth of Britons 'do not Use Internet'" *BBC News* https://bbc.co.uk/news/technology-49607061

11. May, T.C. 1988. "The Crypto Anarchist Manifesto." https://activism.net/cypherpunk/crypto-anarchy.html

12. February 2019 "Blockchain—The Answer to Everything?" *Fair Trade* https://fairtrade.org.uk/Media-Centre/Blog/2019/February/Blockchain-The-Answer-to-Everything

13. Barrett, B. July 2019. "Think FaceApp is scary? Wait Till You Hear about Facebook." *Wired* https://wired.com/story/faceapp-privacy-backlash-facebook/

14. Papazoglou, A. August 2019. "Silicon Valley's Secret Philosophers Should Share Their Work." *Wired* https://wired.com/story/silicon-valleys-secret-philosophers-should-share-their-work/

15. Baucherel, K. 2018. "Who can be Trusted with Our Personal Data?" *Center for Digital Ethics and Policy,* https://digitalethics.org/essays/who-can-be-trusted-our-personal-data

Previously Published Work

Baucherel, K. 2018 "Blockchain: From Hype to Help" *ITNOW* 60, no. 4, pp. 4–7 https://doi.org/10.1093/itnow/bwy087

Baucherel, K. 2018. "Gold! Gold! Gold from the Blockchain River" *Center for Digital Ethics and Policy* http://digitalethics.org/essays/gold-gold-gold-blockchain-river

Baucherel, K. 2018. "Will Big Business Compromise the Ethics of Artificial Intelligence?" *Center for Digital Ethics and Policy* http://digitalethics.org/essays/will-big-business-compromise-ethics-artificial-intelligence

About the Author

Kate Baucherel is a business development and strategy consultant specializing in the application of emerging tech in business, particularly blockchain and distributed ledger technology. She has held senior technical and financial roles in businesses across multiple sectors, leading several enterprises through their startup and growth phases. Kate's first job was with an IBM business partner in Denver, back when the AS/400 was a really cool piece of hardware and the World Wide Web didn't exist, and she has enjoyed the journey to today's awe-inspiring technical landscape. She holds a 2nd Dan black belt in karate and has two children. Kate's writing encompasses the factual and the fictional. Her books include nonfiction digital adoption guide *Poles Apart: Challenges for business in the digital age,* several short stories in the *Harvey Duckman Presents…* sci-fi anthologies, and the SimCavalier series of futurist thrillers including *Bitcoin Hurricane* and *Hacked Future.*

Index

OTHER TITLES IN THE FINANCE AND FINANCIAL MANAGEMENT COLLECTION

John Doukas, Old Dominion University, Editors

- *Rethinking Risk Management* by Rick Nason
- *Welcome to My Trading Room* by Jacques Magliolo
- *Common Sense Finance* by Sean Stein Smith
- *Numbers that Matter* by Evan Bulmer
- *Risk and Win!* by John Harvey Murray

Announcing the Business Expert Press Digital Library

Concise e-books business students need for classroom and research

This book can also be purchased in an e-book collection by your library as

- a one-time purchase,
- that is owned forever,
- allows for simultaneous readers,
- has no restrictions on printing, and
- can be downloaded as PDFs from within the library community.

Our digital library collections are a great solution to beat the rising cost of textbooks. E-books can be loaded into their course management systems or onto students' e-book readers.
The **Business Expert Press** digital libraries are very affordable, with no obligation to buy in future years. For more information, please visit **www.businessexpertpress.com/librarians**. To set up a trial in the United States, please email **sales@businessexpertpress.com**.

Lightning Source UK Ltd.
Milton Keynes UK
UKHW020609130320
360289UK00005B/80

9 781951 527365